The Word Engaged

The Word Engaged

Meditations on the Sunday Scriptures
Cycle C

JOHN F. KAVANAUGH

ORBIS BOOKS

Maryknoll, New York 10545

The Catholic Foreign Mission Society of America (Maryknoll) recruits and trains people for overseas missionary service. Through Orbis Books, Maryknoll aims to foster the international dialogue that is essential to mission. The books published, however, reflect the opinions of their authors and are not meant to represent the official position of the society.

Manufactured in the United States of America

Library of Congress Cataloging-in-Publication Data

Kavanaugh, John F.
    The Word engaged : meditations on the Sunday Scriptures : Cycle C /John F. Kavanaugh.
        p.   cm.
    "Most of this book originally appeared in America magazine" T.p. verso.
        ISBN 1-57075-137-4
    1. Church year meditations.   2. Catholic Church—Prayer-books and devotions—English.   I. Title.
    BX2170.C55K38   1997
    242'.3—dc21   97-6701
                                                                  CIP

In gratitude for my sister, Kathleen Steinman,
my brother, Thomas Kavanaugh,
my father, the late Jack Kavanaugh,
and my mother, Julia Kavanaugh, who gave them to me

Contents

Preface   xi

1.   FIRST SUNDAY OF ADVENT
      A Time of Childhood   1

2.   SECOND SUNDAY OF ADVENT
      Happiness in Hard Times   3

3.   THIRD SUNDAY OF ADVENT
      Joy in the Diminishments   5

4.   FOURTH SUNDAY OF ADVENT
      Stirring in the Womb   7

5.   CHRISTMAS, MASS AT DAWN
      The Centrality of Christ   9

6.   MARY, MOTHER OF GOD
      The Blessing   11

7.   EPIPHANY
      The Child Must Draw Us   13

8.   SECOND SUNDAY IN ORDINARY TIME
      Lovely in Eyes Not His   15

9.   THIRD SUNDAY IN ORDINARY TIME
      Justice Done in Faith   16

10.   FOURTH SUNDAY IN ORDINARY TIME
      Justice Done in Love   18

11.   FIFTH SUNDAY IN ORDINARY TIME
      Open to Transcendence   20

12.   SIXTH SUNDAY IN ORDINARY TIME
      Open to the Supernatural   23

13. Seventh Sunday in Ordinary Time
    Open to the Spirit   26

14. Eighth Sunday in Ordinary Time
    Actions and Orientations   29

15. Ninth Sunday in Ordinary Time
    False Gospels   31

16. Tenth Sunday in Ordinary Time
    Triumph over Death   33

17. Eleventh Sunday in Ordinary Time
    Prayer of Faith   35

18. First Sunday of Lent
    Temptations   37

19. Second Sunday of Lent
    Transfigurations   40

20. Third Sunday of Lent
    Holy Ground of Being   42

21. Fourth Sunday of Lent
    Lost and Found   45

22. Fifth Sunday of Lent
    Resenting Forgiveness   48

23. Passion Sunday
    In Human Likeness   50

24. Easter Sunday
    The Vigil   53

25. Second Sunday of Easter
    Forgiveness   56

26. Third Sunday of Easter
    Peter   58

27. Fourth Sunday of Easter
    After Life   61

28. Fifth Sunday of Easter
    Time and Eternity   64

29. Sixth Sunday of Easter
    Necessary Things   66

30. Seventh Sunday of Easter
    Stephen Martyr   69

31. Pentecost
    The Difference It Makes   72

32. Trinity Sunday
    In the Beginning Was Relationship   74

33. Body and Blood of Christ
    In the Beginning Was Covenant   76

34. Twelfth Sunday in Ordinary Time
    The Gift We Give   78

35. Thirteenth Sunday in Ordinary Time
    Holy Commitment   80

36. Fourteenth Sunday in Ordinary Time
    Blessed Assurance   81

37 Fifteenth Sunday in Ordinary Time
    Freedom on the Journey   83

38. Sixteenth Sunday in Ordinary Time
    Working and Wanting   85

39. Seventeenth Sunday in Ordinary Time
    Praying and Pleading   87

40. Eighteenth Sunday in Ordinary Time
    with The Transfiguration
    The High and Holy Realm   89

41. Nineteenth Sunday in Ordinary Time
    Ancestral Courage   91

42. Twentieth Sunday in Ordinary Time
    Disturbing Faith   92

43. TWENTY-FIRST SUNDAY IN ORDINARY TIME
    Consoling Hope   94

44. TWENTY-SECOND SUNDAY IN ORDINARY TIME
    Reversals of Fortune   96

45. TWENTY-THIRD SUNDAY IN ORDINARY TIME
    Eternal Vigilance   98

46. TWENTY-FOURTH SUNDAY IN ORDINARY TIME
    Prodigal Love   99

47. TWENTY-FIFTH SUNDAY IN ORDINARY TIME
    Problems with Personal Money   102

48. TWENTY-SIXTH SUNDAY IN ORDINARY TIME
    Problems with Corporate Wealth   105

49. TWENTY-SEVENTH SUNDAY IN ORDINARY TIME
    Midwives of God   108

50. TWENTY-EIGHTH SUNDAY IN ORDINARY TIME
    Gratitude   110

51. TWENTY-NINTH SUNDAY IN ORDINARY TIME
    Perseverance   113

52. THIRTIETH SUNDAY IN ORDINARY TIME
    Self-Righteousness   115

53. THIRTY-FIRST SUNDAY IN ORDINARY TIME
    Zacchaeus   118

54. THIRTY-SECOND SUNDAY IN ORDINARY TIME
    The Great Union   120

55. THIRTY-THIRD SUNDAY IN ORDINARY TIME
    The End of the Ages   123

56. CHRIST THE KING
    The Counter-Cultural Sovereign   125

Preface

The scripture engages us when we let it encounter us on its own terms, when we do not fight or fuss with it. If we open the grids of our experience, the Word will be seen and heard, but only through the filters we force it through. Thus it will seem, so often, quite tired and stale. It could not be otherwise, for the sameness we feel is nothing other than the old prejudicial screen which we refuse to relinquish.

If we could hear the Word of God as if it all were new, we might find it too good to be true.

If we could read it as if it were actually real, it might change our lives. We would be engaged indeed.

But that is only half the story, for we cannot escape our proper, private skin. We do not hear the word in some timeless corridor. We do not read it in a vacuum unaffected by place and environs. Whatever is engaged is engaged according to the limits and conditions of the one engaged. True, it is our infinite God who engages us. But it is only we, our poor and graced selves, who can present ourselves to the Word of God. The challenge is this: the more of ourselves we allow to be entered, penetrated, and transformed, the more profound will be the encounter.

These meditations/homilies/reflections over the Sunday readings of the church's "C Cycle" exhibit both sides of the story. There is an effort to yield, to succumb to the truth of God's revelation. Here, the word is read simply as a mystery of faith—something that I might assent to, believe in, hope for, even love—without any particular application to my life or agenda.

But this effort to look at the word as it is, existing outside one's ego, needs, frustrations, victories, and failures constantly gives way to the reality of one's life-world. The two methods join as if in a dance wherein the partners constantly alternate being the lead.

The person who prays must answer the proposal for engagement with his or her own unique "I do."

The person who preaches must weave the words of response from the fabric of his or her experience.

The particular is inescapable. Thank God. For we can only be as particular. And it is the particularities of my own life which so often haunt my observations and perhaps justify yet another commentary on the Gospels.

It so happened, quite unplanned, that the particularities of my response to the Sunday scriptures emerged from a year of witnessing childhood and motherhood, discussing issues of justice and themes of philosophy, coping with temptation, struggling with death, savoring the joys of forgiveness, worrying over the divisions of the church, seeing the splendor of commitment, facing the seductions of privilege, and living with profound loss.

Even more unplanned—and particular—is the fact that my own family so inhabits my engagement of scripture.

Thus the dedication page. My sister, still in her mid-fifties, suffered a series of strokes which threatened life's loss. Her coming back to us, her courage in disability, her uncommonly loving husband and daughter haunted much of my consciousness when preaching or writing of miracle, disaster, or hope.

My brother, with his wife, has taught me far more than the humbling lesson I recount in the reflection for the twenty-fifth Sunday—not only by their freedom and generosity with things, but by their sharing of their three children, now adults, with me and so many others.

My father, dead almost twenty-five years, remains a deeply felt presence, an aura of humor and song, of conviction and strength. He taught me kindly of the holy souls.

And my mother who, by God's kind favor, gave me not only life but the persons above, remains a wondrous image of faith and joyful life over eighty years. She also confirms the conviction of Pope John Paul I that God is a mother to us as well as a father.

All but three of these reflections have appeared in *America* magazine during my second year of tenure writing its column "The Word." They appear now in this volume with the amiable co-operation of Fr. Bob Collins, S. J., and Fr. Philip Fischer, S. J., of St. Louis University's Jesuit community.

.

1. A Time of Childhood

Jer. 33:14–16; 1 Thes. 3:12–4:2; Lk. 21:25–28, 34–36

"The days are coming."

Once the celebration of Thanksgiving was over, I would go to the windows almost every morning, looking for snow. It is one of my earliest memories, a tissue of images held together by feelings that always had something to do with expectancy.

For children of other countries or climates, the prod might not have been Thanksgiving or the thought of snow, but I wouldn't be surprised if the early days of Advent were, for Christian boys and girls, eager ones.

Some children had Advent calendars, others had wreaths decked with candles. Many observed the strangely prophetic feast of St. Nicholas, with its long stockings bulging with many small promises of greater gifts to come.

Songs changed with December. Worldly anxiety combined with hope in "You better watch out . . . Santa Claus is coming to town." The "Dance of the Toy Soldiers" made the spine tingle. And church hymns deepened everything: "O come, O come. . . ." "Wake, awake, the night is dying."

Advent is anticipation. Jeremiah thrives on it: "The days are coming when I will fulfill the promise. . . . I will raise up a just shoot. . . . He shall do what is right and just in the land. In those days Judah shall be safe and Jerusalem secure."

Advent is promise and prayer. Paul's letter to the Thessalonians brims with desire: "May the Lord increase you and make you overflow with love. May he strengthen your hearts."

But the high hopes of both Jeremiah and Paul were electric with apprehension as well. They both wrote in ages of turmoil

1

and threat. Jeremiah felt cold exile and utter loss. Paul wrote to a community besieged by change and alien powers, in words apocalyptic. There was much to fear.

Fears, too, are feelings of childhood. We commence our lives with such daunting vulnerability. The unknown, the unmanageable, the treacherous are everywhere. We await the return of the familiar all the more urgently: the reappearance of the parent gone a mere few hours; the replay of surprise joys we beg our parents to repeat once more; the clinging to comfort when doom approaches.

In another Advent, perhaps my tenth, I saw the face of a child go from death to life. She, a mere three years old, was with her mother on a Christmas-shopping day. In the aisles of an enormous department store she lost the center of her life, who happened to be thumbing through bargains on the other side of the world—an insignificant clothing table away.

The child's temple collapsed. Her face blotched with high shame and sorrow. Sobs erupted with instant convulsion. And then the mother swooped from nowhere to cradle the girl in arms that transformed the shrieks into tears of relief and joy.

Life, from its beginning, bears its gloomy portents. They need not presage the end of the world or even the fall of our mightiest temples. But any child can suspect that all might easily be lost. As Freud reminded us, we begin to die the moment we are a-borning.

Today's passage from Luke's Gospel, the discourse on the destruction of Jerusalem, has Jesus speaking to our hope in the midst of doom. He invokes the imagery of all our primal fears: "There will be signs in the sun, the moon and the stars." Jesus tells of nations in anguish. Seas roar, waves crash upon us. People die of fright.

Darkening skies, longer nights announce the winter of life. But the child in us looks for the sign of love in the sky, the rainbows of fall, the snows that brighten the earth, the arms that reach down to lift us up. We love to light the candle that dispels the dark. We can't wait to open the next window on the Advent calendar.

And so, even with portents of the end times, there is the promise born: We will "see the Son of Man coming on a cloud. . . . When these things begin to happen, stand up straight and raise your heads, for your ransom is near at hand."

Like Israel, like Paul, the childhood we never leave is suspended between devastation and delight. We rise and rush to the window imagining snow. We sit up, alert to songs that promise joy. We attend to the slightest confirmation that our ransom is at hand.

Each ensuing Advent thus reawakens the child in us. And yet, as each approaches and then recedes into the past, our frail childlike qualities mysteriously mature. We slowly come to a realization that there is a deeper hope, a more profound ransom, a truer liberation.

We begin to hope that Jesus Christ's radiance will be brighter than any snow. We start to trust that his light could be more luminous than all the candles ever burned, anticipating Christmas.

2. Happiness in Hard Times

Bar. 5:1–9; Phil. 1:4–6, 8–11; Lk. 3:1–6

"Take off your robe of mourning."

There may be doubts as to the dating and the authorship of the book called Baruch, but the reality it addresses is clear. Jerusalem has fallen, destroyed by Nebuchadnezzar. The book is written in exile, sent from the far kingdom of Babylon. It is a call for repentance, a reflection on true wisdom, and a promise. Despite circumstances of deprivation and desperation, Baruch is a labor of hope.

"For God will show all the earth your splendor." Though stripped of grandeur, Israel will be led by God in joy. Even in their terrible loss, God will shower them with glory, mercy, and justice.

Paul's letter to the Philippians is also filled with promise. A great work has been started in the community, and Paul is convinced that it will be carried to completion. What is more, he is filled with love for them: "God knows how much I long for each of you with the affection of Christ Jesus. My prayer is that your love may more abound, both in understanding and wealth of experience, so that with a clear conscience and blameless conduct you may learn to value the things that really matter up to the very day of Christ."

High hopes and comforting words. But we would miss much of their power if we failed to realize that Paul is writing from prison. Moreover, the little Philippian community addressed with such tenderness and compassion is being besieged by external forces and internal divisions. Paul is in chains and the outlook is bleak, yet this letter is the occasion of some of the most beautiful Pauline passages: the undying affection of the first chapter, the poetic faith of the second, and the exultant reliance on God of the third. Such splendor, but in the midst of such pain.

Luke's Gospel heightens this paradoxical affirmation of hope despite almost impossible odds. Christ's imminent coming is announced, in the first chapter, in the ominous shadow of Tiberius's rule. The Evangelist notes that Pontius Pilate is procurator; Herod is tetrarch; Annas and Caiaphas are high priests—all names that bode more doom than deliverance. These men are the mighty and the dangerous, the important and the awesome.

Yet hidden in the badlands of their dominion, a single voice is raised to preach repentance and forgiveness. John the Baptist, mindful of Isaiah's promise that all shall see the salvation of God, grasps that the time is ripe. Here was this hidden man, John, a voice in the wilderness of time, who was given God's word. "Make ready the way of the Lord."

Beyond the rise and fall of the great nations, lasting longer than all the tinhorn dictators, who has survived? What reality is important? What word has lasted? Whose voice endures?

It is good for us to answer and remember. More than all the victories of the Caesars, the pomp of tetrarchs, and the grandiosity of the highest priests, it was the outsider, the baptizer, who addressed all history.

The truth, uttered in adversity, holds more power than all the huzzahs bellowed in triumph.

3. Joy in the Diminishments

Zeph. 3:14–18; Phil. 4:4–7; Lk. 3:10–18

"Rejoice in the Lord always."

Don't worry; be happy. So we've always been advised on the third Sunday of Advent. Crank up the jollies. Rejoice. Cheer up.

What if you don't feel like it? What if you feel besieged, overworked, overwrought, tired, cramped, and alone?

Sometimes the most useless thing to say to a sad person is "Snap out of it." Yet this is what the Liturgy of the Word seems to insist on. Zephaniah tells a timid, disheartened people: "Fear not, be not discouraged. . . . God will rejoice over you with gladness." Simple as that.

To rub it in, the psalmist, despite our fears and weaknesses, cheerily demands that we cry out with joy, that we be confident and unafraid. You might as well say, "Have a happy day," or pass out smile buttons.

Paul is just as bad. To a bickering, fearful, and restless community he writes: "Be unselfish. Dismiss anxiety from your minds. Just trust our God and present your needs." Then the church, supposedly, will be flooded with peace, understanding, and harmony.

But what if it doesn't work? What if Advent doesn't take? What if things get worse or the pain does not let up?

Advent's themes of happiness and hope can annoy someone who hurts. When you are burdened with the chaff of ego or the weight of anxieties, forced joy and canned glee disgust the best of persons.

Yet it is nothing but our diminishment, our losses, our sadness, our weight of sin that Advent confronts and calls us out of. Somehow it is the pathos of our own melancholy that must be laughed away. It is our sense of exile, our cramped confinement, the dross of our psychic baggage that must be burned off by the fire of love.

The crowds John encountered had, themselves, little reason for joy. Aware of their own need for deliverance, they felt a glimmer of anticipation that he might be the messiah. He counseled justice and rectitude, but the promise he spoke of was something far more than they might have suspected or wanted: "I am baptizing you with water, but there is one to come who is mightier than I. He will baptize you in the Holy Spirit and in fire. His winnowing fan is in his hand to clear his threshing floor and gather the wheat into his granary, but the chaff he will burn in unquenchable fire."

I used to think this passage referred to the contrast between the saved and the lost. My prayer was to be in the happy granary, not burnt in the fire.

But this is clearly a misreading of the Baptist's words. The fire is part of the baptism in Jesus and his spirit. Fire is not the fate of the lost, but the refining of the blessed. We all have our chaff, our dross, our waste. We all have our winnowing. And it is the fire of Christ that will burn it away. The burdens we carry do not make us unfit for Advent's message. They qualify us as prime candidates.

The only exit from Dante's Purgatorio was a wall of fire. Once the pain was burned away by love, the other side was Paradise, sheer joy.

4.   Stirring in the Womb

Mic. 5:1–4; Heb. 10:5–10; Lk. 1:39–44

"Blessed is she who trusted."

Life, like birth, takes time. It has a long gestation. The bloom appears only after a slow unfolding of the bud, wherein every moment of development finally participates in the glory of the full flower. We never quite grasp the process until it's over.

Yet, strangely unlike life, we anxious humans are impatient with process. We are restless with our beginnings, our smallness. It is hard to wait, to trust that something good and great will come of all the mute moments in between.

It is the same with a people's promise. Israel, seemingly condemned to insignificance, was a people called to faith, by the prophet Micah, that God's guarantee would somehow come true. "Bethlehem, too small to be among the clans of Judah . . . from you shall come forth for me one who is to be ruler in Israel." Out of their hidden smallness would rise a mighty and wondrous shepherd whose greatness could span the ends of the earth.

Little Bethlehem had in its midst a smaller life yet, a body prepared for the great high priest, the Letter to Hebrews notes, who would come to do the Most High's will. The single "yes" of this high priest was destined to win the sanctification not only of Bethlehem and Judah but of nations.

What the infancy narratives are all about is a subject of contention. The most considered and delicate judgments can be found in the commentaries of Raymond E. Brown, S.S. Yet no matter what we make of these accounts of Jesus' origins, they reveal that his "yes" was made possible only by an earlier act of trust. The Virgin believed that greatness would be worked out of her own life, her own womb. She believed the promise of God and, in doing so, gave birth to the promise.

The Gospel story of the Visitation is a wondrous convergence of insignificance and portent. Two cousins greet, one running to assist the other, both pregnant with life and faith. The hidden unborn quickens the triumph of faith in Elizabeth who, despite all appearances, recognizes in Mary the mother of her Lord: "Blessed are you among women and blessed is the fruit of your womb. . . . The moment your greeting sounded in my ears, the baby stirred in my womb for joy."

The secret encounter of these hitherto unknown women announces the future course not only of four lives, but of the world.

When I read this Gospel, I often imagine the women of the Visitation; not those two in the hill country of Judah, but those in our midst. They are a religious community that by worldly measure is not only hidden, but too small and fragile to have a future. Yet in the scope of eternity, greater works may be done in their hearts than in the plans and projects of mayors and managers who deem their own roles strategic. Politicians come and go; smug party operatives assume the throne of pride and prominence. But somehow it is the fragile and silent that live on.

And what could be more fragile and quiet than two unborn children? Surely we in this abortion culture know that much. The child before birth is voiceless and vulnerable. Those who are small and insignificant are simply that: not big and not important. They can easily be expunged from our personal thoughts and our political discourse. But with hope, with trust, with patience—gifts of the pregnant mother—life is born again in every child yessed into life.

Any mother who has ever been with child in faith, who has ever been pregnant in hope, has rushed to the friend, the compatriot, the spouse, the family and announced the good news. The promise is terribly precarious. Anything can happen, suddenly, brusquely, and definitively. But the hope remains, and over time faith's long labor yields life.

In some ways, I think, God is most appropriately thought of as a mother. What an act of courage it takes to complete the task. What a demand upon the ego, one's time, one's plans, one's privacy. There can never again be a thought of oneself alone. One's world is now invaded by the invitations and intrusions of the unplanned visitor, the unexpected guest. Pregnancy is the emergence of the other within, an other which is one with oneself, but not oneself. All love is borne this way.

Visitation is not only the paradigm of God in our lives. It is also the way we enter each other.

Our loves and hopes are fragile, growing things. They require nourishment; they take time. Nothing great and enduring happens fast. So we wait; we trust. Could we believe that the promise God wove into our very souls might give birth to something big? Could we hope that something so small and fragile in us could someday walk free and upright and joyous?

The question of every mother who ever birthed a child is the question of our own dear God birthing us, calling us into a precarious existence.

Is it worth it all? "Blessed is the one who believed the promise." So it was with Mary. So it is with God.

CHRISTMAS, MASS AT DAWN

5. The Centrality of Christ

Is. 62:11–12; Tit. 3:4–7; Lk. 2:15–20

"Through Jesus Christ, our savior."

In Calcutta even the poorest Catholic families will find their whitest saris and dhotis or their newest pressed shirts to attend Mass at midnight or early Christmas day. They will file up to the child in the crib who is surrounded by mother and father, shepherds, and friendly beasts.

In Harare, the *Gloria,* song of angels, will be chanted in rich harmony, matching the splendor of color in gowns and vestments. Rich and poor, black and white, young and old in this capital of Zimbabwe will approach the altar to welcome the body of Christ.

In Hong Kong and Santiago, Melbourne and Leeds, Galway and New Orleans, Managua and Prague, lines of women, men, and children will all approach the same Lord to be sustained by his very life.

They will witness the same reality of the consecration in words and languages as diverse as the contours of the earth. And they will honor the same birth of one child in one particular hovel, billions of moments ago, in a village named Bethlehem.

Christmas is a great feast of both concrete particularity and universal import. Christmas is not merely about some Western heritage or ethnic celebration. It is about humanity and the heavens. It is about us.

In Isaiah's promise of the messiah, God speaks to all the ends of the earth. Zion, the old and new, shall be a sign of the holy and redeemed of God. Our psalms are filled with prodigious claims. This king is the joy of the earth, of all the islands. His justice, proclaimed by the very heavens, is for all generations to witness.

St. Paul reminds us quite directly how central Christ is to us and our salvation. "When the kindness and love of God our savior appeared, he saved us, not because of any righteous deeds we had done, but because of his mercy." The spirit of God is lavished on us through Jesus Christ who saves and justifies us. We all become heirs in hope of eternal life.

That the eternal Word of God became flesh is a message as much for the entire world as it is for Jew or Christian. "Glory to God in the highest, and peace to God's people on earth."

What was the event that the angels announced? What was the mystery that God made known to shepherds? What was it that they saw and understood? What was revealed in the baby resting in the manger? What could be astonishing about it? What was there worth treasuring, worth pondering, and praising?

What, indeed, so inspires the human heart here and now on Christmas day, whether it be celebrated in Anchorage or Cape Town? Does it not reach far beyond Europe, far deeper than the thoughts of theologians? Is it not far more wondrous than projections of human consciousness?

Christmas means that God not only created space and time: God entered them, became our flesh and blood, our kin, our child.

There is something here of more than mere sectarian import, more than a cultural fable competing with the other stories of our start and finish. Christmas is a high and holy secret about every mother's child for all time.

6. The Blessing

Num. 6:22–27; Gal. 4:4–7; Lk. 2:16–21

"God sent forth his Son born of a woman."

The writings of St. Paul are insistent and urgent: Christ is strategic to the world. The birth and life of the Lord Jesus are not just more of those events that might or might not have happened. They are the fulcrum of human destiny. By the coming of Jesus we are delivered from the law, and we become adopted children. We are no longer slaves, but heirs. And this is by God's design.

Jesus is how God blesses us, more than Moses might have imagined. In his face God shines upon us and is gracious to us. In him God reveals eternal kindness and wishes us lasting peace. In him we know God's name and appearance and attitude.

We Christians believe that the Psalms sing of Christ in a chorus made of every tribe chanting through the centuries. All peoples have reason to be glad and exult in him. The entire course of history will one day praise God in Jesus. He is the guide of the nations, for all the ends of the earth, for all the limits of time.

Let us look at this child and try to fathom the things that have been said of him, the acts ascribed to him, the hearts given to him. This is no matter for nonchalance. To believe that Mary is the Mother of God is to believe something that is surely either preposterous or miraculous. There is no way we can domesticate this unspeakably wonderful event.

There are some Christians, perhaps dulled by the commonplace familiarity of their own creed, that think it quite an ordinary matter. Others might say that one religion or mythos is as good as another, that ours is good for us, but not necessarily good for anyone else. And yet, if we were ever bold and honest enough to take seriously what we profess, we would realize that the Christmas story is either sheer madness or utterly wonderful.

If it is a fabrication, it is the most hilarious or heinous of mass delusions. But if it is true that the eternal Word of God was born of Mary, then there is indeed good news—not just for us, but for all epochs.

One of us, who walked our earth and lived our life, is the revelation of God. A human brother of ours, born of woman, is God's very child. And since he is our brother, we too become God's children in a new way.

Paul writes to the Galatians that we are adopted by God. Think on this. We are not children of God by natural birth, but by God's desire to choose us, to bring us in. As an adopting parent, God wants to share all goods and grace with us. After Christmas God now looks upon each of us, poor humans in history, and sees the likeness of his only beloved child. The human countenance is forever altered.

And we now—in the Spirit of Jesus, God's only begotten,

who is one with and of us—may raise our eyes to the great and mighty Holy One and say "Abba."

The blessing that the Lord gave to Moses for the Israelites is the blessing that God gives to all humankind, the blessing of the adopting parent who wants only our joy: "May the Lord bless you and keep you. May the Lord let his face shine upon you and be gracious to you. May the Lord look upon you kindly and give you peace."

7. The Child Must Draw Us

Is. 60:1–6; Eph. 3:2–6; Mt. 2:1–12

"The star stopped over the place where the child was."

One of the benefits of giving lectures in different parts of the country is the chance to see both the wide diversity and the deep unity of our faith. Thus, I take every opportunity to attend Sunday liturgy in some local parish of an unfamiliar city.

The highlight for me this year was Our Lady of Grace in Greensburg, Pennsylvania, I felt like I was in on some great conspiracy of life and love: a young girl boldly proclaiming the Word of God, the commissioning of teachers and parents as primary educators, a family of five celebrating its tenth year as they bore gifts to the altar, and waves of believers — grade-schoolers, teenagers and white-haired octogenarians— receiving Communion.

What struck me most, however, was the homily of the pastor, Father Larry Kiniry. He revealed, in a way I had not seen before, how redemptive the presence of children can be in our lives. Not only does Jesus welcome the children, not only does he welcome the child in all of us; we ourselves must do the same.

There is a wisdom in the openness of the child, an insight in its vulnerability. The child must trust us and rely on our fidelity. The child teaches us to forgive and to ask forgiveness. The child seals and expresses our love, our commitments. The child shows us how to play again, how to laugh, and how to hug.

Children draw us together at their baptisms, their first Communions, their graduations. We are proud of them, happy for them. We go to their endless ball games, cheer for them, ache for them, heal their hurts, celebrate their victories. We thrill at the one line they may speak in their first play, the halting melody at their first recital. "A little child shall lead them."

Isaiah dreamed dreams for the child Israel. It is a vision about every child. Splendor. Your light is here. There is the glory of God here. No matter what darkness covers our earth, no matter how thick the clouds, there is a hidden glory shining here, a radiance. We have but to raise our eyes and look about us, to see our sons and daughters, close or afar. They are the gifts and the magic that make our hearts throb and rise with abundance. More dear than the wealth of nations and sea treasure, more lavish than caravans of gifts, more precious than gold, more fragrant than incense, in them we praise God.

God's secret plan, Paul wrote, is that we are all co-heirs of God's glory in Jesus. Every mother's child bears his face. All members of his body share in his promise.

The astrologers, having seen his star, searched for the newborn king. Herod was frightened of the baby. The defenseless child was a menace to something cold and hard in him. He wanted to kill, not see the glory.

In Pennsylvania or Louisiana, St. Louis or Manhattan, in our great parade of parish life, let us go to the child. Like sages, let us delight at seeing the star, at entering the house, at seeing the mother. Let us do homage. Let us open the gifts of our hearts.

SECOND SUNDAY IN ORDINARY TIME

8. Lovely in Eyes Not His

Is. 62:1–5; 1 Cor. 12:4–11; Jn. 2:1–12

"You shall be called 'My Delight.'"

Isaiah is not alone among the prophets in portraying our relationship to God in images of covenantal love. Hosea's Yahweh
will "betroth you to myself forever, with tenderness." Ezekiel
spins a marvelous tale of courtship, betrayal, and redemptive
pardon to explain the history of God's commitment to Israel.

But Isaiah goes beyond the others. He presents an outright
celebration of nuptials: God's relation to Israel, to us, is an
undying covenant of love and fidelity. "You shall be called 'My
Delight,' your land, 'Espoused.' For the Lord delights in you,
and makes your land his spouse. As a young man marries a
virgin, your Builder shall marry you. As a bridegroom rejoices
in his bride, so shall your God rejoice in you."

God's desire and delight is to be one with us, to share in our
life and destiny through thick or thin, to possess the same
Spirit of love over all our miscellany of time and disposition. It
is that Spirit, writes Paul, that we have been given in Christ
and that unites us in body, worship, and common labors.

Thus, it might be more than happenstance that the first
miraculous "sign" of Jesus recounted in the fourth Gospel
occurs at a wedding in Cana of Galilee. Not only does his presence bless the covenant of marriage; he personally heightens
the celebration. Prompted by his mother, who informs him
that there is no more wine and who alerts the attendants to do
"whatever he tells you," Jesus transforms six stone jars of water
into wine.

And it is good stuff. "People usually serve the choice wine
first; then when the guests have been drinking a while, a lesser

vintage. What you have done is keep the choice wine until now." This first sign of Jesus revealed his glory, and thenceforth the disciples believed in him. The glory revealed is that of the great God of transformations, a God who takes a mere creature for beloved spouse, who becomes our food and drink as if our bread and wine.

We have a God who refashions the human body into a temple of flesh inhabited by divine life. We are new arks of the covenant.

Jesus himself, of course, is the greatest sign of all. He, in one body, true God and true man, is the marriage of heaven and earth. He is the nuptials of God and flesh. He is the reason why, after Christmas, every new child bears the one Spirit wherein God calls each one, "My delight, my joy, flesh of my flesh, my spouse." Gerard Manley Hopkins puts it thus in "As Kingfishers Catch Fire":

> For Christ plays in ten thousand places,
> Lovely in limbs, and lovely in eyes not his.

THIRD SUNDAY IN ORDINARY TIME

9. Justice Done in Faith

Neh. 8:2–6, 8–10; 1 Cor. 12:12–30; Lk. 1:1–4; 4:14–21

"Fulfilled in your hearing. . . ."

Perhaps the most constant failure of Christians is our reluctance to take our own Gospels seriously and entirely. We have an uncanny ability to block out those portions of scripture that challenge our prejudices and to magnify those that confirm our own advantage.

A question much ignored these days is whether our faith has anything to do with justice, economics, capitalism, poverty, or other sociopolitical issues. We have pried open a yawning gap between the world of faith and the world of "real" issues. As a result, we never have to worry about changing our behavior or confronting our culture.

Groups often linked to evangelical values provide an odd confirmation of this. Think about it for a moment. What issues are associated with the powerful new Christian Coalition: Forgiveness? The poor? Liberty for captives? Setting the downtrodden free? Caring for the wounded? No, usually these groups are trumpeting their own enlightened self-interest or some other value more rooted in market imperatives than Gospel ones. Even books about "the virtues" and pundits harping about moral decay seem wholly unaware of the spell that capitalism has cast upon us.

This is quite strange for a people that contends that its way is the way of the Lord Jesus. After all, Christ actually began his own ministry, his own preaching under the power of the Spirit, with the great words of the prophet Isaiah: "The spirit of the Lord has been given to me, for he has anointed me. He has sent me to bring the good news to the poor, to proclaim liberty to captives, to the blind new sight, to set the downtrodden free, and to proclaim the Lord's year of favor."

What kind of Contract with America might be generated from such a declaration? What State of the Union might be crafted? Would we hear of belt-tightening for the poor? Tax relief for the middle class? Ridicule of the welfare recipient? Bigger walls to shut out immigrants?

This is not a matter of Democrat versus Republican. Neither party works out of evangelical conviction, unless religion is used to support some ideology of right or left. The common conviction both parties share deeply is about money and self-interest. Even care for the poorest and most threatened among us, the unborn, is moved to the back burner by pragmatists now more interested in capital gains.

That's called politics.

But a politics engaged in by men and women of faith is a

politics shaken and transformed by faith. The words of Isaiah, spoken by Jesus in Luke's Gospel, are supposed to be fulfilled in the hearing of them. We make his words real, we make our faith real, only if we allow it entry into our real world. That is the world of life and love, of people in society, of nations, of economies. Without that entry, Jesus' ministry is enfeebled. Our faith becomes the lazy lap dog of acculturated tastes and seats of power.

There are surely humanistic reasons for opposing the death penalty and abortion, for more fair distribution of wealth and the world's gifts, for the use of talents and expertise in service rather than obscene self-indulgence.

But when a Christian opposes murder on death row or in hospital delivery rooms, when a Christian proposes an economy of service rather than greed, it is not just a matter of human calculation. For us, it is a matter of faith. It is a matter of whether we really believe the words we have heard and the actions we have seen in Jesus, who represents most fully to us God's will and our mission.

10. Justice Done in Love

Jer. 1:4–5, 17–19; 1 Cor. 12:31–13:13; Lk. 4:21–30

"No limit to love's forbearance."

The stirring anthem to love found in Corinthians is most often heard at weddings. Sometimes at wakes.

I typically see tears among parishioners as the litany rolls on. . . . Love is patient, kind, not envious or boastful, not rude. It does not insist on its own way. It is not self-seeking or prone to anger. It does not brood over injuries. It rejoices with the truth. There is no limit to its forbearance, to its trust, its hope, its power to endure. . . .

Perhaps the soul is stirred because we know how easily we fall short of its ideal in our relationships with those we propose to love and presume to mourn. But the tears are also consoling. Most of us have felt those wondrous moments when we tasted its truth; we have sensed the freedom of such love and felt its healing power.

The Corinthian passage is also personally consoling. For we know, no matter what our failings and insignificance, our God, who is love, the writings of John tell us, is ever kind and patient with us, endless in mercy, not prone to anger or resentful brooding.

A staggering thought, however, is that such love should mark the way we live as social beings. Christians must love others as God has loved us. And this, it seems, is a command of screaming impracticality.

There is much meanness in the world. There is much meanness in our culture. Is our faith germane to such a fact? Many say, "No. Keep your faith for pie in the sky, but keep it away from the 'real world' of class, race, nation, gender, and especially money." Love is so alien to our politics, one might seem a simpleton to suggest it has its proper place.

A case can be made that our economic and social way of life is not only joyless, but unkind, impatient, and rude. Arrogance, boasting, and pomposity blight media and marketing. The sneer of in-your-face athletics and television talk shows typifies political posturing.

Not love forbearing, but resentment is parlayed by sectarians who would have us blame the rich, blame the poor, blame the parents, blame the lawyers.

Not love delighting in truth, but a cult of deception marks our social discourse, our slimy videos and exposés, our courtrooms, our Congress, and White House. It is almost as if we presume that we are always being lied to.

Not love enduring, but the endless celebration of unfettered choice and unrestrained accumulation grounds the so-called moral discourse of modern times.

Imagine this. What if there were a politician who could

somehow speak of love? What if there were a President who would not only talk of a kinder and gentler nation but refuse to drop bombs upon a city like Baghdad? What if a people's nobler hopes and dreams were addressed, their latent generosity and fairness, their willingness to share with the unfortunate?

What if there were a liberal politician who could spare as much love for human fetuses as he or she can muster for baby seals and trees? What if there were a conservative politician who realized that words of love apply to criminals and refugees as much as they do to unborn humans and middle-class Christians?

Such a politician would be a person whose professional life was informed by a faith and love that necessarily yields justice.

It would not be easy. Jesus himself, after he announced the good news to the poor, first amazed, then angered his audience. He was too ordinary and too close to give such prophetic utterance. It cannot be real. He cannot be real. Eventually they were filled with rage and wanted to cast him out. So it went when he began his ministry.

How goes it with Christians today?

11. Open to Transcendence

Is. 6:1–8; 1 Cor. 15:1–11; Lk. 5:1–11

"Put out into the deep."

A hallmark of what some academics have called the "postmodern world" is the loss of transcendence. It is supposed that there is no other reality than the projections we humans construct, whether individually or communally. All of existence seems to have been unmasked as a distorted mirror of our passion for power and pleasure.

We do not need some pedant to lecture us on deconstructionism in order to feel its effects. Nor need we realize that the great prophecies of postmodernism are found in Nietzsche's will to power, Marx's money-Molech or Freud's seething cauldron of the id. We see, hear, and smell the theory every day, in our streets, in the courthouses, on radios and television. Power, money, and pleasure reign supreme as the values by which to measure our lives and happiness.

In an unrestrained celebration of choice, the human will is worshiped as the ultimate reality. There is no standard of truth and goodness outside of us, before which our wills must bow. We make the truth. We concoct what is good. And "nobody has any right to tell me what to do." The human will has no duty, no responsibility, no obedience to any authority other than itself.

We think we celebrate openness: but it is an openness only to the projections of our own lips and minds. Rarely are we open to the wholly other—some other that transcends the mirror images of our ego, class, ideology, nation, or any other pet particularity. Our openness is precisely not to transcendence. It is a hankering after our own constructions, those effigies we feel comfortable with, those icons that make us feel secure, those ego-clones that confirm our self-importance.

True transcendence is something else altogether. Isaiah knew he was in the presence of some reality higher and loftier than any human or earthly throne. "Holy, holy, holy is the Lord of hosts. All the earth is filled with God's glory." Isaiah's earthly house shook and billowed with smoke. He became immediately aware of his paltry and sinful condition. This encounter with high mystery, utterly beyond him, shattered any delusion of grandeur he might have had. "Woe is me, I am doomed! For I am a person of unclean lips, living among a people of unclean lips."

The quality of this transcendent experience is uncannily matched in Luke's Gospel story of the great fish catch. After preaching to the disciples and the crowds, Jesus tells Simon to "put out into deep water and lower the nets." Simon's resistance is due to the fact that he and his fellows, for all of their own efforts fishing through the night, have caught nothing. Obviously, there is nothing out there. "But if you say so, I will lower the nets."

Herein is the openness of Peter, despite the meager evidence of his experience, to a will other than his own. And this brought such a great, unexpected catch that even the apostles' resources were at the breaking point. Their fishing nets nearly ripped apart. They caught more than their craft could hold. Their boats almost sank.

In the presence of this superb show of power beyond human reckoning, Peter adores the awesome mystery he has witnessed and is suddenly conscious of his sinfulness, like Isaiah. "Leave me, Lord; I am a sinful man."

The moment we recognize our inadequacy, our sin, our smallness before the greatness of the transcendent God, we are capable of truly being called out of ourselves. When God is heard to say, "Whom shall I send? Who will go for us?" Isaiah responds, "Here I am. Send me." He is empowered, not paralyzed.

Similarly, Christ's manifestation of transcendent power was not for the sake of stirring human anxiety and fear. Christ wants to call us to a life mission far beyond the expectations of our constricted categories.

Human encounter with the transcendent God has always met with resistance. But the idea of a God wholly independent of our sway is especially repulsive to contemporary taste. After all, it requires a terrible admission of our insufficiency. It demands a recognition that we cannot rescue or save ourselves. It commands a yielding to, a humble listening for, an obeying of an other utterly beyond our mere human minds and wills.

The gospel Paul preached rests upon the recognition that we mere humans stand in need of salvation and that we are powerless to do this for ourselves. What is more, we are sinners who need to be healed of our moral wounds. This, we believe in faith, has been done in Jesus Christ, who died for our sins and promises us a world beyond our earth and our earthly projects. It is not by dint of human science, alchemy, or artifact that our meaning can be found. It is only by God's kind favor that we are what we are and that we are made for something far greater still.

If that last paragraph is not an insult to the postmodern mind, nothing is.

12. Open to the Supernatural

Jer. 17:5–8; 1 Cor. 15:12, 16–20; Lk. 6:17, 20–26

"Cursed is anyone who trusts in human beings."

Perhaps Jeremiah was having one of his many bad days when he came up with that bit of wisdom. The very idea. We are cursed if we trust humans.

When we hear such outrageous statements in our scripture, if we're not dozing off, we must somehow flick a little switch in our consciousness that allows us to think, "This has to be nonsense." Then we don't have to worry about making sense out of it in our daily lives. No sane human would think or talk the way Jeremiah does.

But that is what should give us pause. Maybe our sane, human way of thinking is not God's way. What if God's ways are utterly unlike our ways?

We try to enlist God in the respectable ranks of human nature, the best, highest, and brightest of us. But God is not us. God is utterly beyond our words and concepts, infinitely more vast than our deepest desires and resistant to our meager common sense.

Moreover, if we are to judge by Luke's account of the

Sermon on the Mount, even Jesus, who is God with us, has a view of human affairs thoroughly at odds with our own. If we have to tune out Jeremiah's mistrust of humankind, imagine the skills of repression we must employ to ignore Christ's rejection of our every human impulse.

The benighted Nietzsche was clever enough to see the terrible truth in the Sermon on the Mount. What Jesus proposes is a bald reversal of human nature. Nietzsche knew that every last one of us wants wealth abounding and a full stomach. We dread suffering and tears. Being hated, ostracized, and insulted by others is among our greatest nightmares.

But Jesus deemed such conditions blessed. We are to rejoice if we are poor and hungry. We are to take delight in our tears and accept gladly our rejection by the powers of the age. This outright rejection of natural wisdom and desire so infuriated Nietzsche that he raged at those who might dare to follow Christ:

> Not contentment, more power; not peace at any price, but war; not virtue, but efficiency. The weak and the botched shall perish: first principle of our humanity. And they ought even to be helped to perish. What is more harmful than any vice?—Practical sympathy with all the botched and the weak—Christianity.

Nietzsche realized that there is something in Christianity dreadfully at odds with our natural impulse. He would never settle for some watered-down feel-good Jesus who pals along with us in our strutting.

Unfortunately, Christians have done just that. Rather than rejecting outright Christ's teachings, we soften and suffocate them with the pillows of our more realistic wisdom. As the great English writer and theologian Dorothy Sayers observed, we have snared the lion of Judah, trimmed his claws, and turned him into a domesticated kitten.

But if we allow the ways and words of Jesus to have their

full force and vitality, we will realize that there is a higher wisdom that confounds all our categories. It is inescapable. If we are to accept Christ, there is something, someone, wholly other than our nature and inclination. The God incarnate in Jesus, the eternal Word made flesh, points to a reality that can never be reduced to human dimension.

Jeremiah, whether we like it or not, in some profound sense was right. We cannot put our trust in humanity. That, weirdly enough, is the devastating program of Nietzsche. He would have us obey only the pulse of our nature, our will to power. This not only denies the authority of God over us; it denies the claim that any other could make upon our wills. It is my survival against yours.

For Christians, our strength, our hope, is not in our flesh, not bound to the cycles of earth. St. Paul, though less contentious than Jeremiah, says as much. "If the dead are not raised, if Christ was not raised, our faith is worthless." And for Paul, the new life of resurrection was only one indication of the unsearchable and incomprehensible ways of God.

While Christ is the entry of God into our human nature, and so transforms all nature and earth itself, his very being is a message that there is more than our humanity, more than all the orderings of the cosmos.

If there is no supernatural order, the Sermon on the Mount makes no sense. But neither do our liturgies, their holy acts and words. When we come together in worship, we do not merely celebrate and honor our frail fellowship and stories. Nor do we adore the mutations of the natural world. What we do is make present to ourselves the mighty work of God, who is the "mystery tremendous and fascinating."

It is not our task as Christians to conform the Christ of God to our needs and expectations. Our task is to conform our lives to him.

13. Open to the Spirit

1 Sam. 26:2, 7–9, 12–13, 22–23; 1 Cor. 15:45–49;
Lk. 6:27–38

"The first man was of earth, the second is from heaven."

While the mind of Friedrich Nietzsche was unraveling as the last century ended, Freud's was taut, wrapped around the mystery of unconscious human behavior.

Both thinkers are now celebrated as the great unmaskers of motivation. They spread the awful news that we humans are not as nice as we think. Under our seeming civility and tidy-mindedness lurks a raging thirst for power hunkered down around an oven of anger and lust that Freud dubbed the "id." Civilization, to Nietzsche's disgust and Freud's approval, supposedly tamed those feral impulses, yet both men suspected that the cooker of repression would explode.

Politically, world wars and holocausts—as recent as events in Rwanda—seem to have confirmed their frightening visions. In academic circles Nietzsche and Freud are lionized as prophets of deconstruction. And in mean streets, will and power work their ruthless ways.

What does all this have to do with the word of God? It suggests how dissimilar God's word is to our own.

The glow of a new way sparks throughout the story of David and Saul. By most reasonable judgment, David should have finished off his enemy and predator. Saul wanted nothing more than David's defeat. Yet, at the very moment when God had delivered Saul into David's grasp, the chance to drive a final stab to the heart and end the threat, David turned away from revenge and violence. "Do not harm him, for who can lay hands on the Lord's anointed?"

What is only a glimmer in the book of Samuel has blinding brilliance in the Sermon on the Mount. The "anointed of God" is now no longer only the person of Saul. It is every mother's child—even one's enemy. "Love your enemies, do good to those who hate you; bless those who curse you and pray for those who maltreat you. When someone slaps you on one cheek, give the other; when someone takes your coat, give your shirt as well."

Admit it. This is dumbfounding, crazy—at least to our natural attitude. It is so disconcerting to our normal frame of mind, we Christians have learned to distract ourselves with minutiae while we dismiss the revolutionary import of Christ's words.

"Christ-stuff" infuriated Nietzsche. Freud, urbane humanist that he was, was more sober in his estimation, but just as grave. In *Civilization and Its Discontents* he wrote of the ugly truth that people are so eager to deny, that humans are not gentle creatures who want to be loved and will defend themselves only if they are attacked:

> They are, on the contrary, creatures among whose instinctual endowments is to be reckoned a powerful share of aggressiveness. As a result, their neighbor is for them not only a potential helper or sexual object, but also someone who tempts them to satisfy their aggressiveness on him, to exploit his capacity for work without compensation, to use him sexually without his consent, to seize his possessions, to humiliate him, to torture and to kill him. Who, in the face of all experience of life and of history will have the courage to dispute this assertion?

Freud was a deep humanist and a proper gentleman, but he saw in himself and all of us something atrocious. He therefore spun out the predatory logic of organisms bent on maintaining their natural existence.

But as Paul writes to the Corinthians: "The spiritual was not first: first came the natural and after that the spiritual. The first man was of earth, formed from dust, the second is from heaven." Dust, after all, is a thing: it-ness, matter, the it, the "id." And Freud fully excavated the underground of human existence if there is nothing to us but dust, if we are mere "its." He found only the cruel grind of natural processes, laws of consuming and entropy, the big eating the small, the powerful crushing the weak.

Yet Christ is the second Adam, the second David, the new Moses for this remnant of Israel which calls itself a people of the new way and covenant. And his new mountain of teaching can never, ever, be interpreted as a product of human pretense. Nietzsche and Freud have taken that route as far as it can go, and it leads to a trash heap of history.

Jesus Christ is flesh, yes, but Word of God made flesh. Henceforth all human flesh is reordered and reconstituted. Something wonderfully new has been done in us, taught to us, given to us. The more we yield to it, the more we will be empowered, freed from fears of losing or disappearing, loosed from chains we thought our only security in an unsafe world.

Is it too high, too difficult to aspire to the Sermon on the Mount? Will we not fail? Is not the risk too great? What shall come of us when we dare to give it all away?

However, if we believe our prophet, we need not cower before the odds. The God we worship is even more wondrous than the way offered.

"Be compassionate, as your father is compassionate. Do not judge, and you will not be judged. Do not condemn and you will not be condemned. Pardon, and you shall be pardoned. Give and it shall be given to you. In good measure, pressed down, shaken together, running over."

14. Actions and Orientations

Sir. 27:4–7; 1 Cor.15:54–58; Lk. 6:39–45

"When a sieve is shaken, the husks appear."

A topic of contention in moral theology today involves what has come to be known as the theory of the "fundamental option." One viewpoint, considerably simplified here, maintains that there are a number of human actions so grave that they indicate the entire state of soul of a person in relationship to God. Sometimes this has been associated with the notion of mortal sin, an action weighty enough to determine a person's eternal destiny.

The other side stresses the life-orientation of a person, a fundamental option, which is not necessarily summed up in any particular human act, even one that in itself might be considered grave. Thus, someone basically oriented to doing God's will might break a solemn marriage vow; and yet this might not mean that the person has totally lost the state of grace. A particular moral act need not indicate that the sinner has wholly rejected the will of God.

Neither side of the debate will see this description as fully adequate. But that is not new. Neither side ever seems to feel that the other side adequately reports its view. This was evident in the response, for example, that some theologians gave to Pope John Paul II's criticism of the fundamental option in his encyclical, *Veritatis Splendor,* on moral theology. The Pope stressed that with every freely committed mortal sin a sinner can lose sanctifying grace, charity, and eternal happiness. Some critics deemed this a harsh and rigid emphasis on particular choices which misunderstands the full meaning of "freely committed" actions.

The scriptural images of the tree and the fruit it bears may offer a way out of the impasse. The homey wisdom of Sirach reminds us that even our speech reveals who and what we are. Like the fruit of a tree, the words of a person disclose the kind of mind the person has. We are advised not to evaluate people until we hear their words. In fact, the only way we come to know anything or anyone is by observing their actions.

Jesus, in the Gospel of Luke, also turns to the image of the tree. "A good tree does not produce decayed fruit any more than a decayed tree produces good fruit. Each tree is known by its yield." Good persons produce goodness from the goodness of their being, evil from their store of evil. Our acts flow from our being, St. Thomas Aquinas taught us. Gerard Manley Hopkins put it: "The just man justices."

Clearly then, our actions reveal who and what we are. It is impossible to separate the actions a person does from the person who does them. So those who insist upon the significance of our actions to determine our moral status have a point, especially if they are speaking of acts we do with sufficient reflection and freedom.

"Each of us speaks from our heart's abundance," Jesus tells the disciples. But can the heart's abundance be revealed in one act? Possibly, but who can tell? It seems that I can summon up as much self-knowledge and self-ownership as humanly possible and give myself to good or evil in a particular act. But when and where this happens is a mystery perhaps inaccessible even to the wisest of us.

What we can be sure of is that we are all sinners. There is a store of evil in all our hearts, the Gospel says. There is a store of good as well. Perhaps this is why St. Peter, who, we might presume, heard these words, would never give up hope in Christ's forbearance and forgiveness, no matter how weighty and catastrophic his moral failure—cowardice, lies, even betrayal.

I think this fact is often missed by antagonists in the fundamental option debate. Some seem eager to prove that people are, indeed, condemned to hell. At times their opponents seem equally eager to prove that none of us could ever deserve that. I propose that we all might merit it, but all could well be saved —especially if we are open to the fact that we need salvation and if we call upon the Lord's name in repentance.

What Jesus often warns against is the danger of judging, not actions, but the human heart. And even in today's Gospel, he reminds us of a truth more basic than our ethical disputes, one which we too frequently forget.

What if all sides of all theological controversies, including the fundamental option debate, lived out the words that Jesus spoke to crowds that sought to touch and follow him?

> Why look at the speck in your brother's eye when you miss the plank in your own? How can you say to your brother, "Brother, let me remove the speck from your eye," yet you fail yourself to see the plank lodged in your own. Hypocrite, remove the plank from your own eye first; then you will see clearly enough to remove the speck from your brother's eye.

15. False Gospels

1 Kgs. 8:41–43; Gal. 1:1–2, 6–10; Lk. 7:1–10

"I have never found such faith. . . ."

Sometimes, as Solomon praying in the temple knew, the most effective prayer may come from an unexpected or "foreign" voice. Although we often presume that those who hold our tenets, bear our name, and share our heritage are most like us in faith, it is not always the case. It could well be that those who nominally seem like us are less like us than those who are deemed "other."

I fondly remember conversations with my wonderful professor of philosophy, Dr. Albert William Levi. When I was working on my dissertation concerning Hegel, Marx, and Marcuse, Professor Levi seemed most concerned that my faith not be shaken by such dangerous luminaries. "Not to worry," I said to some effect. I told him that I thought there was a profound bankruptcy at the bottom of their worldviews. It had to do with the absence of love.

As it turned out, it became clear that my nonchurched Jewish professor and I had more in common than either of us had at first suspected. It seemed strange to him that he felt more solidarity with me than with many atheist humanists. And it seemed strange to me that I felt closer to him than I did to many Christians. I know that he was drawn to Catholicism ("The only faith that I am attracted to," he said). But he judged that his conversion was neither requested of him by God nor a fitting disposition to his Judaism, which he did not want to finally reject.

With respect to my relationship to other believers, perhaps I felt a bit like Paul, who wondered if the Galatians were deserting the cause of Christ "and going over to another gospel." Paul insisted that there was no other gospel, even if an angel from heaven should preach it. Yet it seemed to me that some Christians followed "gospels" which were more economically, politically, or sexually accommodating than that of Jesus. Levi, however, shared that spirit of Paul which showed no desire to please humans or ingratiate himself with them.

The Gospel presents a centurion who sends Jewish delegates to Jesus on behalf of his sick servant. ("He loves our people and built our synagogue.") This nonbeliever says, "I am not worthy to have you enter my house." And Jesus responds: "I tell you, I have never found so much faith among the Israelites."

And so, sometimes, I do not find in the "New Israel" the quality of the faith that I found in Levi. So strangely have people fashioned a gospel for themselves, they seem to think that such sentiments as "God helps those who help themselves," "Charity begins at home," and "Cleanliness is next to godliness" are from the Gospels. (They are more likely from Ben Franklin.)

As opposed to these meager moralisms, Levi had a deep unspoken longing and hope that God might indeed be revealed to us. Shortly before he died I asked him, "Well, Bill, are you open to all the Truth there is to be known? Are you open to all the Good there is to be loved?" He knew exactly what (or Whom) I was speaking of. And he said, "Of course!"

It seemed a profound openness of heart, probably as stirring as the faith of a Roman Centurion who, one day, thought himself unworthy to be the host of Jesus.

16. Triumph over Death

1 Kgs. 17:17–24; Gal. 1:11–19; Lk. 7:11–17

"No mere human invention."

Elijah begged God to restore a dead son to a poor widow. Guilt was the order of the day. She presumed it was either Elijah's fault or her own that the son had died. But the guilt was overcome. The prophet, hovering over the lad, called his life-breath back.

Jesus, for his part, encountered a widow at Naim. He saw her in the funeral procession of her only son. Moved with compassion for her loss, his words were, "Do not cry." He touched the litter and said, "Young man, I bid you, get up." Then Jesus gave him back to his mother.

But did these two children of two widows eventually die someday? Of course they did. This can only mean that the message behind all those accounts of bringing back to life is not the perpetual postponement of death. Death will come, whether now or later. But the healings of the prophets, as well as Jesus, are symbolic of a deeper healing. The point cannot be to stave off death. If that were the point, Jesus himself should never have died.

But Jesus did die. And he was risen up by the power of the Father. That is the point. No matter what death we endure—even sin itself—it is not definitive. We are reborn in Christ.

I am reminded of a conversation I once had with a neurologist who was working at an internationally renowned medical research center. As we were walking by a huge urban cathedral, I mentioned to her that many of her colleagues would deem the church nothing more than a monument to our fear of death. "They might," she said. "But the real monument to our fear of death is the place I work."

This is one of the paradoxes in the vaunted rhetoric of the Human Genome Project. It is presumed by the evening news that somehow we might discover all the genes that make us susceptible to death. But it is organic life which dooms us to death. We might even live, purified of cancer, Alzheimer's disease, and cystic fibrosis propensities, but we will die nonetheless. Eliminate all of the environmental hazards—secondary smoke, sun exposure, and all the permutations of salt and sugar—and we will still die.

There is no physical practice, no spiritual mantra, which will elude the fate of biological existence. The only hope is that there is some nonbiological source of our being which sustains us and will guarantee our endurance.

The miracles of our scriptures are not the occult promises of some eternal life on this planet. They are, rather, signs of our destinies beyond it. They are promises that the God who made this earth is not subject to the limits of it.

We are not made for nothingness after death. But we ourselves, no matter what the brilliance of our achievements, no matter what the possibilities of the Human Genome Project, cannot avoid death's finality. All of our efforts are the glories of human inventiveness, but our faith and our Gospels are not the results of our deliberations.

As Paul writes, the gospel is "no human invention." Nor is it received from any human tradition or schoolish training. It is nothing if it is not the revelation of a God who transcends human artifact and human death itself, a God who calls us to share in that eternal life, "by revelation from Jesus."

17. Prayer of Faith

2 Sm. 12:7–10, 13; Gal. 2:19–21; Lk. 7:36–50

"I have something to propose to you."

I once thought the most boring parts of the scriptures were the overt stories and parables. I was drawn, rather, toward those parts of the holy writings which were outright commands or at least recommendations. These moral statements were clear and direct. They were stirring. They challenged one's idealism. They revealed the way one should live.

I eventually happened upon a spiritual director who refused to allow me to apply the scripture as a map for my journey. In the retreats I made with the late Paul Quay, a Jesuit priest, he told me not to apply any of the scriptures directly to my life or the issues which I thought were most important to me.

"Just look at the text in faith. Ponder it but do not apply it to yourself in any way. Listen to it. Observe it. Give yourself to the story. See if you can confirm what is going on. Witness it. Affirm in faith that you believe the truth of the passage; that is enough. And, only if there is something that emerges from the story that moves you, let it happen."

It was a frustrating venture. I liked the moralisms and the challenges straight and pointed. Yet my director would not let me apply the stories to my life. "Keep yourself out of it," he said, "unless it breaks into you."

Despite my initial resistance, I found a secret wisdom in this prayer in faith. And it was revealed in the very methodology of the scriptures.

The prophet Nathan went to David, not with an indictment, but with a story. Since it was a parable, David was not on his guard as he listened to the tale.

There were two men. One was rich and the other poor. The rich man, despite the great number of his abundant flock, gave to a traveling visitor, not one of his own sheep, but the prized single lamb of his poor neighbor.

David was outraged at the story. He demanded that the offender give restitution or even be put to death. Only then did the prophet tell him that the story was about himself. And only then was David able to see his crime against his friend Uriah, whom he had murdered, and his wife Bathsheba, whom he had taken as his own. In the story repentance was achieved.

Our resistance to repentance parallels our resistance to love. If we experience ourselves unable to fully trust that God could love us unconditionally, the indirect method of parables sometimes is the most effective strategy to help us accept the mystery of our own redemption.

In the Gospel story, the way that Jesus chose to unmask the self-righteousness of the Pharisee was to tell a story. He did not directly challenge his host, who was scandalized by the sight of a sinful woman cleaning the Lord's feet. Rather, he told the tale of a debtor who was forgiven great debt.

Only then did he directly address the host with the reality of his situation. While the host had done nothing but condemn a poor sinner, that very sinner had knelt before Jesus, washed his feet, dried them with her hair—all because of her great love.

We often see the truth better in the stories of others than we do in ruminations about how well or how poorly we are doing. Whether we are people who judge or are people who think we are hopelessly sinful, we must enter the parables of

Jesus, as with all scripture, with the prayer of faith that my old director recommended.

If we give ourselves to the mystery revealed therein; if we come to say, "Yes, I believe that you could love her in such a bountiful way," we might then hear the words spoken to us that were once said to David. "The story is about you."

18. Temptations

Dt. 26:4–10; Rom. 10:8–13; Lk. 4:1–13

"Not by bread alone."

How shall we deal with the awesome contingency of our lives? We so much want to make a difference, to leave our mark. Yet we know we disappear into the vast reaches of space and time. We die and go to ashes. Such is our creaturehood.

Ernest Becker wrote in *The Denial of Death* that the preeminent human temptation is to escape or repress the truth of our frail skin. We avoid the desert, the loneliness, the loss of familiar support, the grand stillness. If we go into the wilderness, we will be reminded of the great hunger. We will be dwarfed by the earth's mighty movements.

Enter distraction. If we keep ourselves ceaselessly preoccupied, we might be spared the pain and the pained. We need not pay attention to the terrible precariousness of our condition. We need not embark on the quest for an answer to our absolute lack. Perhaps if we entertain ourselves to death, we may be able to divert our way through life.

A tempting tactic: turn the stone into bread. No more yearning for the fullness. We can have it at our beck and call. By the snap of our fingers we fill the hole at the bottom of our being.

Another option: power. If we could only control and dominate, then we need not fear the terrors of the night. And if that fails, we might devise some magic. The splendiferous event. Defy the laws of human gravity, the pull of earth. Scale the treacherous heights unharmed.

The temptations Jesus underwent were to escape from the mission of his humanity, to deny our dependent condition. Let him dodge the mortality he supposedly took upon himself. Let him be everything but human. He could take the world by storm, by the sheer force of impressiveness. After all, if he could turn stone to bread, what faith would we need? (He would, as a matter of record, change bread into his body, but only for eyes that see in the full risk of faith. Imagine the hosts of spellbound believers approaching the altar to receive a little homunculus body now formed out of bread: Shazzam! What an act!)

Why did he not, by command, grab all our empires by the neck, dwarfing Alexander and the Caesars? Our timid allegiance could be exacted, squeezed out of us. Why did he not dominate, grandiose earth king, our wobbly wills? Then he need never rely on the free gift of the human heart. He would just enchain it. He could recreate us in a new image: rigid robots, awestruck automatons. Imagine him, flying in stupendous spirals around our cathedrals. Surely he would be *Time*'s man of every year. The biggest newsmaker imaginable. Let him be a superman or Captain Marvel, not a person of flesh and blood. Not a human whose whole sustenance would be the word of the one who sent him.

Jesus entered not only the desert, but the hunger as well. He was unguarded in the wilds of time, powerless before the raging logic of unleashed appetite. He was so embarrassingly common and little, so like us in every way but our sin, our escapes, our lies, our refusal to be what God made us to be.

He resisted the seduction. And the evil spirit left, to await another opportunity. It would appear again when the love would become almost unbearable, the wounds of our humanity agonizing. Finally, when he walked with us into the desert of our godforsaken dying, he gave us not escape, but those few reliant words of passage, "Into your hands I commend my spirit."

In some strange way, Christ utters the same commendation to us. He will not dazzle us. He will entrust his saving of us into our hands for free acceptance. As Dostoyevsky's Grand Inquisitor in *The Brothers Karamazov* complained, this was Christ's big mistake. We would rather have the easy bread and showy circuses. We would prefer the domination of rigid authority over the terror of our free "yes" to him.

It is easy not to like Jesus' proposal for our salvation, since it requires us to enter with him yet more fully into our creatureliness. He offers no way out from our wounds. He only gives us passage through them. And, halting before the journey, we are again tempted by the inquisitor's questions in the desert.

As for Dostoyevsky's Grand Inquisitor story, Jesus remains quiet in the face of the tyrant's reprimand that the mission has been all wrong. Jesus does not silence the liar. He does not cast the fraud from his throne. He merely kisses the man's cheek and goes back to the streets of history, searching out the prize for which he came: the free gift of a human heart, the commitment in faith, the acceptance of his passion, death, and resurrection.

No, neither bread nor magic will save us. It will be only, as Paul writes, by our entry into Christ's own act of total trust and abandonment, believing in our hearts that therein we ourselves are raised from the dead and delivered.

"Everyone who calls upon the name of the Lord will be saved."

19. Transfigurations

Gen. 15:5–12, 17–18; Phil. 3:17–4:1; Lk. 9:28–36

"We have our citizenship in heaven."

Although we rarely pay attention to it, a great paradox haunts our practices of Lent. We go through these six weeks every year fairly easily; yet if we stopped to reflect seriously on what's going on, it would be a shock. To our liberated American souls, it might even seem like an earthquake.

Just look at the imagery and themes of the period. Lent starts with ashes and a warning: "Remember that you are dust and to dust you shall return." It prods to repentance: There is something wrong with us and the world. I am not O.K.; neither are you. We are insufficient. This life is not enough. Each of the six weeks brings a profound admission of our inadequacy.

This is not easy stuff for a world given to excuses and plea-bargaining. The most we admit to is making a mistake or perhaps behavioral problems. But to admit that we are in profound trouble? Why? We all know there is nothing so terribly wrong with us.

Even some of our hymnals have rewritten an old song here and there to mollify our tender egos. I've caught myself doing the same, balking before the admissions of "Amazing Grace." I've thought of rephrasing it: something like " . . . how sweet the sound that saved a nice fellow like me." Come to think of it, singing that I was once "lost" and "blind" seems to be overdoing it a bit.

Lent ends with an equally unpalatable celebration of cataclysmic failure: betrayal, brutality, cowardice, and degradation. True, it is reversed in a triumph of joy and glory, but in a way that defies all the laws of common sense. The dead, crucified one rises, his wounds glorious.

What is Lent trying to rub our faces in with all the talk of mercy, forgiveness, reform, and repentance?

We here in the real world know that we are all really rather nice guys and gals. Sure, we make mistakes now and then. But who's to blame us for our fumbling? And surely no one of us would ever deserve such a thing as hell. (I know the polls say that most Americans believe in hell, but the vast majority can't imagine themselves being there.) Surely we are not in such desperate need as the drama of Lent seems to suggest. Surely we do not need someone to die for our sins. Some of us do not even know what such a strange concept might mean.

Why do we need salvation? Why do we even need God, especially if our stomachs are full, our insurance policies paid, and we live and die with the dignity appropriate to beings that can manage their lives tidily, think straight, and at least in some ways be smart and productive?

Lent reminds us that we settle for too little, expect too little of ourselves and of God. Even the earthly promises which God made to Abraham challenged his narrow and routine attitude. Abraham had to look far beyond himself, to the sky and the stars, to imagine a future beyond all his reckoning.

When it comes to accepting the cross and the resurrection, the confines of comfort are even more stretched. We almost have to make the cross something routine and uninteresting. It is an assault upon the delusion that things are going pretty well and that we can settle down to business as usual.

What does it mean to be an enemy of the cross? Paul says it has something to do with having our bellies as our gods. More directly it means being locked into the things of this world. "As you well know, we have our citizenship in heaven; it is from there that we eagerly await the coming of our savior, the Lord Jesus Christ. He will give a new form to this lowly body of ours and remake it according to the pattern of his glorified body, by his power to subject everything to himself."

There is another world, a higher realm, a kingdom not of this earth. There is someone other than ourselves whom we must listen to and obey, since he is the Word of God, the new lawgiver, and prophet, even more than Moses and Elijah. There is more than our frail bodies and the dust from which they came. Other bodies await us, more grand and glorious than the ones we have now. We are not the final word. Nor is our death.

Lent requires a tremendous psychological disengagement from our earthly prejudice. It is nothing but gibberish to a materialist mind. It is madness to anyone whose ultimate goal is to satisfy physical appetite.

But the meaning of Lent rests upon such a transfiguration of our minds and hearts. Its gestures and words require that we believe there is something, someone, for us beyond the stars and the everlasting hills. Otherwise Lent is poppycock.

Perhaps it was for these reasons that Paul wrote to Philippi and to all the denizens of earth, those he could so "love and long for, my joy and crown. Continue, my dear ones, to stand firm." Not on the earth, but in the Lord.

20. Holy Ground of Being

Ex. 3:1–8, 13–15; 1 Cor. 10:1–6, 10–12; Lk. 13:1–9

"I AM sent me to you."

Today's reading from Exodus was a favorite of my favorite philosopher, St. Thomas Aquinas. The story reads simply enough, but for Aquinas the implications were momentous.

Moses is tending the flocks. He sees a burning bush which is not consumed, and he hears his name called out from the blaze. When Moses responds, "Here I am," he is warned to "come no nearer." The spot on which he stands is holy ground. He encounters the God of Abraham, Isaac, and Jacob, the God who has come to rescue his people. Yet Moses is hesitant: "If they ask me 'what is his name?' what am I to tell them?" God says, "I am who am. This is what you shall tell the Israelites: I AM sent me to you. This is my name forever. This is my title for all generations."

This section of Exodus begins an account of the relationship between God and the Israelites. Their God will be a God of free covenant, a God who personally intervenes to save them. "I AM will always be with them."

True, there were other formulations that referred to God, for example: "The Most High," "The One Who Sees," "The Eternal One." And even this particular expression has been given various interpretations, ranging from "I will be who I will be" to "I will be what I was."

But Aquinas saw in the burning bush a revelation of the deepest mystery of a God who could never adequately and accurately be named or conceptualized. There is no other way to talk about who and what God is other than to say that God is existence itself. Am-ness. God is the holy ground of being. At the bottom of the universe is not some mindless grinding machinery or evolutionary process. What moves everything, from stars to human hearts, is personal existence.

If you just think about it, the fact that there is anything at all is the most wondrous thing. Existence is the giver and gift of all gifts. Nothing could be known, if there were nothing to know. Nothing could be loved if there were nothing to love. There could be no fulfillment, no desire, no truth, if there were no "is."

Thus, in Aquinas's own great exodus—his theological and philosophical journey called the *Summa Theologica*—after offering his five ways to God, he centers on existence itself as the word that can most adequately be applied to God.

Existence is the primary value, the fundamental good, one with the very being of God. And since all other beings have their own existence by gift of God, our existence is our primary value and goodness. "Everything that exists is, as such, good, and has God as its cause." If we exist, and we cannot give existence to ourselves, we must have been willed, loved into existence.

God not only creates and sustains every existing being; God also creates each kind of being there is. Every being participates in a hierarchy of goodness and intrinsic value. Each species is good, not only because it exists in the first place, but also because of what it is. Each species brings its own kind of goodness into the world; and each species lost would be a loss of goodness. All creation, in all its myriad forms, is existentially good.

Aquinas valued personal reality as the "most perfect grade of existence" because it images the "I am-ness" of God: life that knows itself and gives itself to the other. This is not some glib speciesism, which degrades other kinds of life. It is just an acknowledgment that freedom, intelligence, and love introduce a new splendor of intrinsic goodness and value into the world which, without persons, would be bereft of such beauty.

But the existence of personal creatures like human beings also introduces a host of problems to the world. Our peculiar goodness as humans is not only a function of the fact that we exist and that we exist as a special kind. We also present a moral goodness to the world, since we, with our capacities for intelligence and freedom, are able to know and possess ourselves and consequently choose to become the kind of persons we become.

Evil, for Aquinas, has no reality in itself. It occurs only as a parasite. Evil appears only because good things exist.

Physical evil is a deficiency or lack in the physical reality of various kinds of beings. Thus, a horse might not be fully good as a horse because it is lame. A fig tree is physically evil to the extent that it does not bear the fruit of what it is.

Moral evil, however, is a deficiency or lack in the kind of human being you or I have freely chosen to be. It is a negation of our truth. It is a rejection of our goodness. It is a radical lie about existence.

All too speculative, perhaps. But might not these philosophical ruminations unlock the mysteries with which Lent ends? That bright vigil will recall for us the holy ground of being: In God's own image, male and female, God created us. And like the great cosmic march of species, we, humankind, were pronounced good by the one who gave us the gift of being. Seduced by the great deceiver, the liar of liars, we seem to have rejected it all. But by the bountiful grace of "I am with you," even the fault itself became a happy one.

21. Lost and Found

Jos. 5:9–12; 2 Cor. 5:17–21; Lk. 15:1–3, 11–32

"Everything I have is yours."

I believe it was the first directed retreat I made. Until then, our eight-day yearly Jesuit retreats consisted of four or five conferences a day, delivered by a preacher and mulled over by us retreatants.

Now I had a director who would assign me readings from the scripture and expect me to report how my five hours of prayer developed as the days went on.

I had found a dissatisfying pattern to my preached retreats. Somehow, after the third or fourth day (usually crowned by a yearly general confession), I seemed not to know what to do. My work, I felt, was over. My life was tidied up. All I could do was wait for the retreat to end.

Although my director for the private retreat did not like the idea of a general confession, he eventually relented on the sixth day. My work, once more, was done. Or so I thought.

What this guy did was give me five more meditations on sin—after the sixth day! And what a day it was.

I remember clearly resenting the fact that I was still thinking about sin when things should be winding down. Here I was being forced to muck around some more in my own depravity, and I was beginning to seethe. My philosophical study of atheists like Jean-Paul Sartre began to haunt me. I had read in his play *The Devil and the Good Lord* that the existence of God degrades the existence of humanity, and I was now suspecting that Sartre could be right.

As day turned to evening, I found myself resisting the whole notion of sin. What's the point of such negativity? Sin. Sin. Sin. God seems to exact from us a degrading admission that we are dirt, junk. The more I thought about sin, the more it nauseated me. The more I reflected on God's mercy, the more I was turned off by it.

At this point I started to worry about my resistance. To be honest, I began to wonder whether I really believed in God in the first place. Well, rather than face that abyss, I concentrated on an old prayer which hitherto had always calmed me down. "O God, you know me and you love me." That would do the trick.

But it didn't. I got more resentful at God. And more worried that I might not even have faith in God.

After an hour of fret called meditation, a little variation on my prayer came to mind. Say: "O God, you know me and you love me; and it's not because of anything I have ever done or accomplished."

Now, dear reader, I do not know where that idea came from. But I hated it. Every time I approached uttering the final clause, I gagged. "It's not because of anything I have ever done or accomplished. . . ." I just could not say it. It seemed as if everything would fall apart if I did.

My efforts don't count? Then why not have an affair, abandon my vows? Why not kill somebody? Didn't sacrifices count? Didn't my hard work matter? Then why on earth have I been trying so hard? If what I've done or accomplished doesn't earn God's love and salvation, then why have I been trying to do the right thing?

"I've slaved for you. . . ."

The story of the prodigal son invaded my memory. That second son. The son who slaved. The son who resented the father's forgiveness for an ingrate brother who botched everything. The son who would not join the party. The son whose father pleaded. The son who complained.

"For years now I have slaved for you. I never disobeyed one of your orders, yet you never gave me so much as a kid goat to celebrate with my friends. Then when this son of yours returns after having gone through your property with loose women, you kill the fatted calf for him."

Somehow I knew my sin as I had never known before. Yet, oddly, I felt God's love with startling newness and equal intensity. "My son, you are with me always, everything I have is yours. But we have to celebrate and rejoice. . . ."

When hearing the story of the Prodigal Son, we often think of the compassionate father waiting at the gate or the desperate son planning his confession in advance. But might there not be a second child in all of us? We work hard, we manicure virtues, we collect the graces, we notch up victories. And we forget what is already ours. The gift, the grace, the kingdom, the love not earned but lavishly given. Before long, our labors become slavery, our accomplishments, chains

I thought if I would ever say a prayer like, "You know me and you love me, and it's not because of anything I have ever done or accomplished," I would surely stop working.

As it turned out, the next year I worked harder than I ever had before. But that year, it was less from fear and more from joy.

Luke reminds us that the parable of the prodigal was told to Pharisees who complained about Jesus eating with tax collectors and sinners. Now, in relief, I thank God for such a banquet.

22. Resenting Forgiveness

Is. 43:16–21; Phil. 3:8–14; Jn. 8:1–11

"I have come to rate all as loss."

Her face is still clear in my mind, even though I haven't seen her for fifteen years and she quite possibly might be gone from our earth by now.

She seemed to have lines that at one time had often smiled, but when I encountered her after Mass one day, her face was all scrunched up like an oversalted pretzel. "You know what I hate about the Gospels," she said, not in a question, but with the authority of more than eighty years. I didn't know quite how to respond, other than to say, "What?"

"The eleventh hour. Those people who come in at the eleventh hour and get paid the same as those who have been working all day. It's like sinners who loaf all their lives and then ask God's forgiveness at the end and get into heaven."

There was no doubt she was angry about the unfairness of the situation. But what bothered her most was the fact that Jesus' parable of the laborers was truly dangerous. If we dared believe it, we would all stop trying and would give up our efforts at being good. It seemed to be saying that our good works were worth nothing in the end.

Well, she had a point. But even at age eighty or eighty-five she had a lot to learn. She was sincere and earnest, no doubt a hard-working person; but I've often thought over the years that if she has died and gone to her reward, she has found a Lord far more wondrous than our meager deals and imaginings. What a stupendous surprise it must have been to encounter Christ the judge. Everything else, our sins or our victories, must pale in comparison.

Paul, in his letter to the Philippians, writes of the overwhelming importance of knowing the Lord Jesus. Nothing else seems to matter. "For his sake, I have forfeited everything; I have accounted all else rubbish so that Christ may be my wealth and I may be in him, not having any justice on my own based on observance of the law." This must have been quite an admission from such an activist and hard worker as Paul. He was willing to count all of his efforts and labors as trash. From this point on, his justification would be through faith in Jesus, not in works.

It would seem, then, if Paul really believed this, he would become the greatest of quietists. Why not fritter away the rest of his life? But the exact opposite happens. Instead of giving up on his efforts, Paul works all the harder.

It is not that I have reached my goal yet, or have already finished my course; but I am racing to grasp the prize if possible, since I have been grasped by Christ. I do not think of myself as having reached the finish line. I give no thought to what lies behind but push on to what is ahead. My entire attention is on the finish line as I run toward the prize to which God calls me—life on high in Christ Jesus.

Unlike Paul, most of us expend our energy for lesser things. We try so hard, not only to win the game of life, but to merit eternal life itself. We think our efforts count so much; we hack away at our salvation. And we may well resent it when others find forgiveness. Perhaps we rise in harsh judgment against those who cannot or will not meet our standards. Perhaps we even condemn ourselves in our failures, embracing the cruel verdict.

What do we do when we nab the adulterers of the world or the adulterer in our hearts? Do we want to stone them? What penalty will we exact of the sinner around and within us? Jesus says, "Let the one without sin cast the first stone." While we rush to judgment and condemnation, Jesus does not. "Neither do I condemn you. Go and sin no more."

This may be a troubling thought. The forgiveness seems too fast; our efforts at virtue seem not to count. Indeed, this is a new way, a new path through the sea of life. Isaiah foretold it: "See I am doing something new. Now it springs forth, do you not perceive it?" The psalmist sang, "The Lord has done great things for us, we are filled with joy."

In Jesus there really is something new that unites us all: the young woman one day long ago caught in sin, the old lady after Mass resenting the laggards, and even the mighty achievers like St. Teresa of Avila. She insisted that her greatest consolation was in the thought that, upon her death, she would meet Christ in judgment and have no virtue or gain of her own to offer in self-defense. She would simply throw herself upon his abundant mercy.

Some of us will just stand there, like the adulterer, in grateful awe and silence. Others, like the dear old lady I met years ago, might find their faded laugh lines restored to haggard faces.

And all of us will celebrate those who turned to him in the morning of life just as much as we cheer on stragglers who had nothing else to offer but their hope, even at the eleventh hour.

PASSION SUNDAY

23. In Human Likeness

Is. 50:4–7; Phil. 2:6–11; Lk. 22:14–23:56

"Into your hands."

"I dread Good Friday this year." It was an honest and simple statement from the gentle woman sitting before me recounting her faith's journey. Yet she spoke not only for herself. She bore some weight we all carry when faced with the prospect of the Passion.

How like Jesus himself, I thought. He desired to eat the meal but dreaded the thought of drinking the cup. When the awful time came, he was as clear and straightforward as the reluctant woman who feared Good Friday: "Father, if it is your will, take this cup from me; yet not my will but yours be done." He tasted the anguish. He bled with worry.

But as Isaiah foretold, this God-with-us would not turn back. He remained unshielded before the siege of life and death. Face set like flint, he clung only to the one who sent him.

God, having made us in godly image, made God in Jesus the likeness of humankind. The incarnation and its inevitable result would be a great emptying out into us. It would be the second fall: the fall of God into our human estate, a sublime bankruptcy with no golden parachute.

It is our human circumstance, grand and grotesque, that is at issue in the Passion. Our predicament is the healing of the wounds without the cover of cosmetics. Our problem is the solving of sin without endless stratagems of denial. "Not guilty," we all say, having taken the ploys of the courtroom as our method of life. We plea bargain our way through while the slaughter goes on. Lacerations we bear in quiet. Cruelties we have inflicted go unmentioned. Deprivations we share in common are unnoticed.

How could any human being ever live and escape the Passion? We would never rear children, never be born, never inhabit such a dear world fraught with peril, and we would probably never grow. Certainly we would never love. It is for us that Virgil mourned the "tears of things." Jesus said more: "Do not weep for me," he advised the women of Jerusalem, "weep for yourselves and for your children."

And so we do in our own passion. We weep for ourselves in abundance or deprivation. We weep for the children we never had and the children we have brought to birth. The tears are inescapable, no matter how hard we might try to pretend otherwise. No power of Pilate or pleasure of Herod can preserve us.

My friend who so dreaded Good Friday had it quite right. It is an inevitable, dreaded season of life. We die our thousand deaths. We pour out our hearts and tears for our young, mourn the lost beloved, the broken companion, the unraveling parent. We sweat the love and bleed the sorrow.

If only there were a way out.

But unexpectedly, wondrously, the one who need not have been like us, yet chose to be so, did not flee. He entered the garden of Gethsemane to rectify the garden of Eden. Not clinging to the robes of divinity, he took the towel to wash our feet. And we, with Peter, might murmur, "not just our feet, Lord, but our whole being, our pains and terrors, our aging and fading, our agonies and death."

C. S. Lewis wrote in his *Poems* that love was as warm as tears: unsettling, uninvited, cleansing, and comforting. It was fierce as fire, flickering with life, smoldering with rage, constant as some eternal flame. Love, too, was as fresh as spring, new and alive, daring and bold. But he ended this song of Love with the most telling stanza of all:

> Love's as hard as nails,
> Love is nails.
> Blunt, thick, hammered through
> The medial nerves of One
> Who, having made us, knew
> The thing He had done,
> Seeing (with all that is)
> Our cross, and His.

Perhaps it is that cross we dread. We'd rather go some day, bright, shining, and unstained, before the broken servant to thank him for his pains, not for us, but for all those others out there who needed it. We would manage our salvation by our efforts and achievements. "Thank you, but, all the same, I'd rather not need such terrible proof of love."

But the dream of sinlessness sours to nightmare when we fail and fall. Having counted on flimsy virtue that cruelly betrays us, in our horror we conclude that we were not even worth the Passion and all is lost. The Pharisee who did not need salvation is joined by the failure who judges himself hopelessly beyond its power and grace.

Good Friday's wood, on which hung the Savior of the world, remains waiting for our kiss. It bore the one who says to us, now and eternally, from the cross: "Yes, you needed this. And yes, you were worth it."

24. The Vigil

Gen. 1:1–2:2; 22:1–8; Ex. 14:15–15:1;
Is. 54:5–14; 55:1–11; Bar. 3:9–15, 32–4:4;
Ez. 36:16–28; Rom. 6:3–11; Lk. 24:1–12

"The story seemed like nonsense, and they refused to believe it."

Light and Goodness. Let it be. Heavens and earth, day and night. Movements of moon and stars that would never have been, had they not been willed into existence. Water, sky, and earth. The great parade of natural kinds, nurtured by earth, fills the horizons. Waters teem and trees flower. Fertility. Multiplicity. Creeping creatures, urgent and easy, wild and gentle, small and great. God is the original environmentalist, the first cause of all our species, the eternal lover of diversity. Good. Yes.

Then the final good gift. "God created them in God's own image; male and female God created them." This final nature, a human one, would be given all else: as gift to nurture, name, and affirm. All is benefaction, and the human, made specially in the likeness of God, is empowered to know existence and pronounce it all good. All is benediction.

At least one might have thought so. But the creature with the power to name, with the freedom of "yes," said "no." It was a rejection of the great order and the great orders. There would be a resounding "no" to the goodness of limits. The tempter was a liar. They already had the tree of life as their shade and comfort. They would not die anyway. They were already like unto God. And yet, resistant to the very condition of their creaturehood, they ate of the tree of limits. They wanted more than the power to name all the goods of the earth. They wanted to name evil, to dictate right and wrong. They wanted to control all, even if it meant losing everything they were.

In exile, there was left to them either despair or faith in a journey back. But such a journey could be led only by one who knew the way, only by one who could be absolutely trusted, one wholly other than the namers who misnamed it all. Thus Abraham, against all hope, learned to place all hope in the promise that God made, to yield and obey at the core of his very being. Thus he became the ancestor of all faith, even in the face of total loss.

The return was rife with peril, traps set by alien powers. Our people were horrified by the odds. The sea of frenzied life seemed impassable. Yet steadfast Moses, armed with nothing more than the "other's" promise, split the very sea in two, offering passage. He became the ancestral leader of all journeys.

The return had its snares, captivities of every manner. Our forebears, like us, knew days and years of being lost and abandoned. Moved by our affliction, the one who first pronounced us good consoles us in prophetic voice. "With great tenderness I will take you back . . . with enduring love I will pity you." The covenants of Eden, of Noah, Abraham, and Moses will never be forgotten.

Something new is promised: a water, not of chaos, but of cleansing; a new food of unremitting nourishment; a mercy confounding, lavish in forgiveness; love beyond the grasp of mere human imagination. "For as high as the heavens are above the earth, so high are my ways above your ways and my thoughts above your thoughts." God's very word will come to be the final "yes" of goodness.

But what of our sin, our resistance, our ritual of death and folly, the compulsive repetition of Eden's inhabitants? How might the wisdom of God penetrate our thickness? If our hearts would only turn, Baruch chides us, with the humility of the stars. If our minds might only surrender to the will that moves the earth. Yet we cling to other gods, their twisted principles and precepts.

Ezekiel, who saw our horrors and shame, indicted us but also promised that the covenant holds despite our deed. Unfaithful, we stay cherished. Besotted, we will be purified. Hard, cold, and lost at sea, we heard Ezekiel's rumor of our ransom. Could we chance a hope for some new spirit, for hearts no longer made of stone, for a homeland?

Who would have guessed that our home might be a person? Who would have dreamed that the passage through the sea was just that: going into the water, even under, but with someone who, like a sleek, glorious dolphin of grace, would bear us on his back?

Jesus entered the deeps of death, a plunge he need not have made, had he not loved us in our sorry state. But he went to death with a "yes," with the utter trust of Abraham, the constancy of Moses, the bright reliance of Isaiah. In Easter's vigil, we plunge with him: "Are you not aware that we who were baptized into Christ Jesus were baptized into his death? Being like him through likeness to his death, so shall we be through a like resurrection."

The risen crucified one sounds again God's original "yes" to us now, even in our sin, even in the death which sin brought on us. Allowing us to be like and in him since he became so fully like unto us, he carries us, as one of his own, to safe land.

"If we have died with Christ, we believe that we are also to live with him. His death was death to sin, once for all; his life is life for God."

25. Forgiveness

Acts 5:12–16; Rev. 1:9–13, 17–19; Jn. 20:19–31

"As the Father sent me, so I send you."

Everywhere the apostles went after the resurrection, they seem to have carried the message, "Peace be with you." Despite resistance to their proclamation of the Messiah, they found new power to work signs and wonders. The sick were cured, the troubled were healed. The events of Christ's Passion, death, and Resurrection were the sign of his undying ascendancy over every threat of worldly dominion. Revelation's rhapsody played through their zeal. "There is nothing to fear. I am the first and the last and the one who lives. Once I was dead but now I live—forever and ever."

We are led by the Gospels' resurrection accounts to think that such confidence was not there from the start. The followers of Jesus, despite the reports of his rising, were locked in a hidden enclave, struck with fear.

It is in this context that the final appearance of Jesus occurs in the body of the fourth Gospel. His words, twice spoken, brought the peace that the disciples would later proclaim to others, for he was sending them to bring good news just as the Father had sent him. "Peace be with you." Then he breathed on them and said: "Receive the Holy Spirit. If you forgive others' sins, they are forgiven them; if you hold them bound, they are held bound."

Forgiveness, and the peace that comes with it, is one of the great themes of Jesus' mission. By this he was not only announced to the world; it was also his final gift. In his teachings, he called us to forgive seventy times seven times, and he fashioned parables of lavish pardon. Forgiveness was portrayed as so central to our lives that it was almost as if our refusal to

forgive could somehow harden our hearts. The unforgiving
heart languishes unforgiven, incapable of receiving forgiveness.

The prayer Jesus taught us in the Sermon on the Mount
instructs us to say, "Forgive us our trespasses as we forgive
those who trespass against us." We say it at every eucharistic
liturgy, as we prepare for Communion.

Have you ever been struck by the irony in the way we can
so effortlessly receive the body of Christ, having prayed the
Our Father, while we carry clinkers of resentment in our
spirits? I wonder if that is why the power of the Eucharist
seems so diminished in us. We walk heavily to the altar,
unaware of the surging mystery around us. If we only believed
the words: "Lord, I am not worthy, but only say the word and
my soul shall be healed." This asking for and giving of pardon
will unlock something in us. Forgiveness frees. Without it, we
are stuck, caught, bound down.

Have you ever heard a father, knotted with rage, say
through clenched teeth, "I will never forgive my child"? Have
you ever seen a wife, heavy with invisible chains, say, "I will
never forgive him again."

I can remember nights spent, dry and restless, after having
wounded another, in such stark contrast to those evenings
when I had the courage not to let the sun fully set upon my
anger.

I can remember dawns, awakening with the dusty grind of
being held unforgiven by another. I woke brittle, like honey
gone hard. Unwillingness to forgive is something we carry like
a weight. The whole world becomes heavier as we become
sterner.

But there is a lightness, a suppleness, in forgiveness. Breathing is easier, fresher. When we forgive, we tap perhaps the
deepest of our powers, to create something new out of nothingness. When we are forgiven, it is as if the world no longer
wars. Demilitarized zones are unneeded. The suspicious, tenta-
tive glance disappears, and the delicate balance of power
dissolves. Disarmament occurs. "Peace I give to you."

Yet peace, like forgiveness, must be received with open

hands. The only way to get unstuck is to be lifted up and out. So it is with the mystery of the Lord's passover. God's love for us, even in our sinful state, is there for the asking if we only believe. We must accept the lavish gift we have not earned. And the more deeply we receive his gift, the more freely we give it. Once we are filled by forgiveness from God, we know how appropriate it is to offer it to others without their earning it.

The Apostles, notwithstanding the shame and the fear, finally believed this. All is made right: wounds, loss, confusion. And having tasted the sweet abundant joy, there was no other choice but to shout it to the heavens, to bring it to the nations, to share it with an incredulous world. The fruit of the Resurrection was their community of faith, hope, and love, their church of Jesus' way. Word eventually got around: "See how they love one another."

THIRD SUNDAY OF EASTER

26. Peter

Acts 5:27–32, 40–41; Rev. 5:11–14; Jn. 21:1–19

"Do you love me?"

Peter in the Acts of the Apostles, so bold and courageous, testifies, "Better for us to obey God than men!" Even with strict orders not to preach, in the rattle of menace from high priestly interrogation, he remains intrepid. He proclaims the risen Lord who "brings repentance and forgiveness of sin." Despite further threats, Peter and his companions leave the arena, happy that they were worthy of ill treatment.

How did Peter ever get over his failure? Such a calamity. The embarrassment alone should have incapacitated him. Three times, we are told, he denied even knowing Christ. (In my earliest school days, this somehow seemed the greatest crime.

The Russians—or Romans—would come, breaking down our doors. All we would have to do to win safety was deny that we were Catholics, deny Christ. With such a high standard of faith, would we even have allowed the likes of Peter into our classroom after his betrayal?)

Peter, nonetheless, must have been used to failure. Even his first admission of sin brought not rebuke from Jesus but, "Follow me." So he followed. He later scaled the heights. With his famous profession of faith—"You are the Christ, the son of the living God"—he got his name: Rock, the sure foundation. Had Jesus been a bit ironic? Within moments, Peter was refusing to accept Jesus' destiny. Not Jerusalem and death! No ignominy! It will never happen! The rebuke was enough to stop a truck. "Get behind me; you have the thoughts of Satan." But Peter, who was perhaps too thick to register the reprimand, just got behind Jesus and continued to follow.

His thickness, or maybe the fact that he was used to his own inadequacy, allowed him to continue following, even after the catastrophe of his denial and his Lord's death.

They navigate the sea of Tiberius, Peter and the gang. "I'm going fishing." How must he have felt, especially at that instant when he and his fellows were challenged about their fishing? The voice from the haze undoubtedly breached a dike of memories from earlier days. "Children ["Lads," the Knox translation puts it], have you caught anything to eat?"

As before, there was nothing. And as before, the sheer power of Jesus' presence was felt on the waters. When they cast the nets on the other side, there were so many fish they could not haul in the catch.

On hearing "It is the Lord," Peter plunged into the water to find him once again. Next we see the fire, the fish and bread, the disciples still stammering about who he might be. Then come those wondrous words spoken to Peter.

"Simon, son of John, do you love me more than these?"

"Lord, you know I love you."

"Feed my lambs."

"Do you love me?"

"Feed my sheep."

And yet a third time, "Do you love me?"—which, we're told, hurt Peter. I wonder why.

"Lord, you know everything, You know well that I love you."

Pause a moment. There is something great stirring here. Have you or I ever uttered those words to another? "Do you love me?" Most of us, once beyond childhood, are terrified at the thought of asking such a question. It is hard enough for some men to tell the beloved she is loved. But it can be excruciating to ask, "Do you love me?" How often have teenagers, sometimes eager to profess their love, been found to ask whether they are loved. To ask it. Has one ever asked a friend as much? A brother or sister?

I could think of scores of questions Christ might have put to Peter. Do you promise never to betray me again? Will you finally be more modest in your claims? Do you now, at long last, after having denied me, amend your life? Will you please modulate your vaunted professions of faith? Now do you see why I had to wash your feet? Well, big-mouth?

But none of this. This God-made-flesh is interested in one thing, the heart and face of the one before him. The gift of a person, even tarnished, so like unto glory it was the only image of God that God allowed. The human "yes." The affirmation, uttered in all its hurt and frailty. The turning of the spirit that won back God's very heart to the Israelites time and time again. The movement of will that quickened Mary's fiat. The surge of hope that rises with every human longing.

Jesus said only, "Do you love me?"

What manner of God is this that we worship? What wondrous love has become incarnate to live and die in Jesus Christ? What splendid manner of man was he? How could we not "glory" in such a God?

The Book of Revelation chants, "Worthy is the Lamb. . . . To the one seated on the throne, and to the Lamb, be praise and honor, glory and might, forever and ever."

It turned out just as Jesus said. Peter became the kind of man who learned to glorify such a God even in his death.

27. After Life

Acts 13:14, 43–52; Rev. 7:9, 14–17; Jn. 10:27–30

"All who were destined for life everlasting believed in it."

As lively and supple as our imaginations may be, some of us draw blanks when we entertain the possibility of heaven. We are so time- and matter-bound that all our visions of another world are necessarily chained to images of this one.

"Will there be ice cream in heaven?" Thus might grade-schoolers echo the question put to Jesus: "Will there be marriage in heaven?"

In the Book of Revelation, the imagery is more grand and ambitious. Whether visionary or dreamer, the narrator awes us with a scale that embraces every nation, race, and tongue, arrayed in long white robes, bearing palms before the throne and the Lamb.

"These are the ones who have survived the great period of trial; they have washed their robes and made them white in the blood of the lamb. . . . Never again shall they know hunger or thirst. . . . He will lead them to springs of life-giving water, and God will wipe every tear away from their eyes."

But how can we adequately conceive of life everlasting, the destiny of those embraced by Christ's life and dying? The Acts of the Apostles announces the promise of an afterlife but does not give much description of what it might be like. And Jesus, in many passages in the fourth Gospel, reminds us: "I give them eternal life and they shall never perish."

We can only guess what such a life might be, and all our guesses will be freighted with limits of the life we now live. Moreover, the limits of earth-bound experience cannot help but foster skepticism about any future life.

In my philosophy classes, when the talk turns to our final fate and the immortality of the soul, a web of unbelief is quickly woven. "How can an 'after' life have any continuity with this life when all our experience is so brain-based? Our memories, our joys, the delights of every sense, the faces of our loved ones all seem so inseparable from this world and our bodies." A telling point. Even mighty Aquinas mused that a soul, separated from the body after death, would somehow be radically incomplete, bereft of the body it informed. Surely, if we had no body, we could not speak of personal immortality. Billy and Mary are not "souls"; they are embodied souls. For Aquinas, happily, his Christian belief in the resurrection of the body answered the nagging questions of reason. Not just our souls, but our bodies are promised eternity.

This does not make things very much clearer. What on earth could such bodies be—supposedly outside of space and time? But that's just it. They are not on earth. And the earth cannot adequately contain their reality.

To my students, then, I pose a thought experiment. Imagine us in a class-womb. We are a remarkable group of fetuses who are aware of and can talk about our condition. What troubles us is the regular and inevitable departure and disappearance of our brothers and sisters. It seems a dread experience, not only for the one who is untimely ripped from our comfortable state but for all of us. We never see them again. They're gone. All that is left for us is mourning and memory.

The question is then posed. Could there be an afterlife, a form of existence beyond this womb, so familiar and secure? Could there be another world beyond the walls of our experience?

One budding philosopher-fetus, clearly on the route to skepticism, deems it impossible. How could there be life after womb-death? Every means of sustenance—oxygen, blood and nutriment—is gone. The cord is cut. How could there be an existence without it? Every piece of evidence we have indicates that we could have no life without it.

Unfortunately, the fetuses who have passed away, do not (maybe cannot) come back to tell us what happened when they died to us and our world. They cannot report what happens on the other side because of the limitations of our life-womb, barring their direct entry to our lives.

But let's pretend. One does return to give an account of the other side.

I know you have a wonderful life here, but this is only preparation. You say that life without a womb is impossible, but that is only because of the womb's boundaries. You think that there could be no food or oxygen without the umbilical cord. Yet there is. Believe it or not, you will receive food, but it will be through your mouth. And your mouth is for much more than mere sucking, breathing, or eating. You will speak and sing, kiss and cry. And your arms and legs will do more things than you could ever imagine with your kicking and swimming around. The new world beyond your womb is connected to what you are right now, but it is wondrously different. All the gifts you have are only glimmers of what they will become.

Could it so be with us? Are we all aborning? And do those slight but awesome moments of ecstatic love and luminous insight only hint at what eyes have never seen and ears have never fully heard?

28. Time and Eternity

Acts 14:21–27; Rev. 21:1–5; Jn. 13:31–35

"A new heaven and a new earth."

The chairman of the philosophy department at Creighton University, John Patrick Murray, was telling me how Augustine's *Confessions* had deeply affected him during his semester's teaching. We were in a diner near the St. Louis airport during his four-hour layover en route back to Omaha. So as the world spun on about us, jets overhead carrying thousands to temporary destinations, the two of us sat in a booth discussing eternity.

Augustine, if you give him your mind for a while, writes with such focused intensity about the things of heaven that by the time you get to the last books of the *Confessions*, you cannot help but wonder: Does the eternal extinguish the importance of the temporal? Do created goods pale, even disappear, in the light of God's resplendence?

Book Nine of the *Confessions* presents Augustine and his mother, Monica, discussing the meaning of death just hours before she herself will depart from earth. She seems so willing, even eager, to let go of this life. They share a vision of eternal wisdom, so splendid as to wash out all other sights, so vast as to dwarf all lesser joys. God, in eternity, would ravish, swallow, and engulf us in eternal blessedness. "Son, for my part, there is nothing now in this life that gives me any delight. . . ."

Why then the "mighty grief" that flowed through Augustine's heart and poured into his eyes when she died? "My soul was wounded, my life rent in two."

Being here, alive, amounts to so little, and so much. We know our dreadful lack only because we cherish our lavish gift. It is all so passing, yet so precious.

And so I mull over my own life, its bounding joys, its wrenching tears. In my mid-fifties, I often feel ready to go, especially if it means a union with everything my heart has ever desired. Yet I cling to this little life, its sweet goodness, its faces, laughter, and song. Embarrassing as it is to admit, a simple cold can trigger fears of mortality now too close.

I am stabbed today with news of a young cousin and his death, at the age of five, on an icy road. A life is so terribly fragile and ephemeral; its loss so devastating. Nothing I might say can ease the anguish of his father and mother. St. Paul advises me, as he did his disciples: "We must undergo many trials if we are to enter into the reign of God."

Yet I, with Augustine, am disconsolate. Being here on earth is wondrous and the threat of losing it is grievous. I hesitate to believe fully the dream of the Book of Revelation. "The former heavens and former earth had passed away, and the sea was no longer. I also saw a new Jerusalem, the holy city beautiful as a bride. . . . This is God's dwelling. . . . He shall dwell with them and they shall be his people, and he shall be their god who is always with them. He shall wipe every tear from their eyes, and there shall be no more death or mourning, crying out or pain, for the former world has passed away."

Will the tears of loss be gently dried, the pain dissolved in celebration? Will God indeed make all things new, bright, beautiful and alive again? Will all the good and grace of a young unfinished man or the enfeebled ancient be preserved?

It is our love that clings to the present, that cherishes all the disappearing goods. Our love, as Augustine says, is part of the love which makes all things to be. The works of time, even our very lives, were from the beginning pronounced not only good, but very good, very lovable. It is only natural that we should love them, even in their frail state. Our very love for the goods of this earth draws us to the good whose self is love. And the God who loved all goods into being abides in that love for all eternity.

Was this the glorious message of Jesus? That the good, and our love of it in all its forms and faces, is the final as well as the first word? That the child's unfettered laughter rings forever, charming the earth yet enduring beyond it? That the wise and gentle endurance of the old will not dissolve as the body falls away? That the love evoked from us would last, and that the love he came to give us is for this life as well as eternity?

Yes. It is our faith that God made all things and makes them all anew in the risen Lord who gave us this command: "Love one another. Such as my love has been for you, so must your love be for each other."

When we fear and grieve, time seems to drag cruelly. We delight, and it hurtles by, uncaring. We shall never grasp the meaning of time and its preciousness, or eternity and its promise, if we do not learn to love.

There is a verse, so common it is attributed to many authors, which goes:

> Time is too slow for those who wait.
> Time is too fast for those who fear.
> Time is too long for those who mourn.
> Time is too short for those who rejoice.
> But for those who love,
> Time is eternity.

29. Necessary Things

Acts 15:1–2, 22–29; Rev. 21:10–14, 22–23; Jn. 14:23–29

"Unless you are circumcised you cannot be saved."

Some people from Judea were causing problems in Antioch. They were insisting upon stringent requirements for salvation. Paul and Barnabus appealed to Jerusalem, after which a settlement was reached. The new Gentiles were not to be upset or disturbed. They were notified that, under the guidance of the Holy Spirit, the young church was "not to lay on you any burden beyond that which is strictly necessary."

What was necessary? Abstention from meat sacrificed to idols, the non-consumption of blood and the meat of strangled animals, the avoidance of illicit sexual unions.

Now that is interesting, not only for what is mentioned, but also for what is not. To be sure, the community of Jerusalem was presupposing dedication to the cause of the Lord Jesus, but they were also reluctant to pile obligations onto their new converts.

What about strangled animals and blood? Are these still prohibited? What about idolatry? Might there be some contemporary parallel to this, when animals are slaughtered and sacrificed for the golden calves of money and power? If these practices are currently permissible, have others taken their place in the catalogue of what is strictly necessary?

One can read in the First Letter to Timothy that women ought not to speak in the assembly. The Letter to Titus, for its part, directs that bishops must be of irreproachable character. They ought not to be heavy drinkers or money-grubbers. And they should be married only once—their children solid believers and properly respectful. Now that's a new twist on the celibacy debate.

On the other hand, what are the practices today that we deem strictly necessary? Inclusive language? Latin Masses? Male homilists? Short sermons?

One of the most seductive temptations of the believer is to identify the will of God with the will of the believer, and not the other way around. God's will is squeezed into patriotism, leftism, capitalism, feminism, hierarchy, civil law, financial success, ecclesiastical tradition. In extreme cases, the supposed will of God can be harnessed to justify leaving a spouse, breaking a promise, even killing someone, whether Communist, criminal, or oppressor.

The same delusion has occurred when philosophers have

mauled the eternal and necessary "law of nature" on behalf of cultural prejudice, class interest, or personal preference. Natural law has sometimes been used to justify the most horrendous of crimes. More often it has been manipulated to legitimate slavery, domination of women, and the exploitation of the poor.

Among the churches, has it ever been heard that a certain practice can never be changed, since it is the will of God? And yet, has the practice been much more significant than the act of circumcision? Clearly circumcision was an important issue. But some of the antagonists seem to have given it the status of unchangeable law.

When I was a novice, a supremely confident novice in the year ahead of me made the pronouncement that two things would never occur. These impossibilities were: a Roman Catholic liturgy in English and a Roman Catholic president. So much for prophecy.

How do we escape fooling ourselves? How do we avoid servitude to merely human laws while we neglect the law of God? How do we guard against the tendency to worship our temporal and cultural fabrications?

Jesus, in the fourth Gospel, promises the Holy Spirit to instruct us in everything and remind us of all he revealed. Is this what led the Jerusalem community to forswear putting heavy burdens on its new believers?

It is Jesus and his word that we ought first and always to remember. Thereby the Holy Spirit instructs us. When we look at Christ, primarily in scripture, it is clear what he is saying: We need repentance; salvation is offered us in his redeeming death and resurrection; and we are called to imitate him in our mission to the world. We likewise encounter him in our community, the church, which from the beginning has given us his word. The scriptures came from the community, under the blessing of the Spirit. So also came our foundational creeds. Moreover, our holy sacramental signs recall and re-enact Jesus' saving power.

Our hierarchies, traditions, teachings, and laws all help us remember. Our holy ones, called saints, and our pieties, called devotions, have ever called us back to his truth. We also see him, as he promised, in the least of our brothers and sisters.

While no one of these can contain all of the mystery of Christ, taken together they are a concert of witnesses to the Easter message.

But one bright truth we should never forget. All ideologies and requirements, all popes and rituals, all theologians and mystics, all laws and traditions, would mean nothing to us as Catholics, if Christ is not risen and has not saved us.

It was no more than good sense to drop circumcision.

30. Stephen Martyr

Acts 7:55–60; Rev. 22:12–14, 16–17, 20; Jn. 17:20–26

"I am coming soon."

The figure of St. Stephen, the first martyr, emerges in the Easter season just as it does in the days after Christmas. I wonder if there is some kind of ironic warning here. Do we realize what we're getting ourselves into when we so readily celebrate Christ's birth into our world and then his Paschal mystery?

Stephen was a deacon, a person "filled with the Holy Spirit and wisdom." Utterly open to and reliant upon the victory of Christ, his was a radical discipleship. His murder, which Acts recounts, was the result of a withering challenge he made to those who resisted the message of Christ. In effect, he took on the leaders of his time. It was enough to get anybody killed anywhere.

Perhaps we've all learned more prudence in accommodating to our cultural ideology and its high priests. There is not much of a market for prophets and martyrs when one is getting along so comfortably with the powers and dominions. Could this be the reason why there are so few voices like Stephen's ringing boldly and courageously in our midst to challenge our nation and society?

It would be an unusual thing to hear some young Christian's voice rise above the chorus of diversity and admit: "Well, I believe that human sexuality is sacred and that sexual love is for married lovers; and I am willing to defend my position." Stephen, where are you?

Or imagine, in the midst of a violent culture, the public profession of a pro-life position that opposes euthanasia, capital punishment (our latest fascination), abortion, and covert military operations—and is not intimidated by the rhetoric of right and left.

Or think of a Catholic university, in this season of graduations, that would not fall all over itself for the opportunity to present a degree to Henry Kissinger or President Clinton. Would there be any questions raised as to whether such an action might be in conflict with crusty institutional credos?

Maybe we've lost our need for martyrs, or at least our stomach for them.

"Don't be such a martyr." Some Catholics may remember hearing this rejoinder when they pouted as children that they were not getting their own way. Others may remember the martyr complex, that unhappy state of consciousness just short of paranoia, in which they thought everybody was against them. Martyrdom may have gotten a bad name from the self-pity and paranoia that could be associated with it. But such associations are unfortunate and impoverishing. Martyrdom is anything but self-indulgent and grandiose. Stephen and other martyrs knew there was something worth dying for (not killing for, which seems to be a more appealing application)—namely, the Christ. If Christ is indeed the Lord of history, "the Alpha and the Omega, the first and the last, the beginning and the end," then it is not a matter of indifference how he lived and what he taught. The many martyrs of our history wanted to give their witness to the world.

We might be more inclined to keep it quietly to ourselves. Faith, we're told, is a private thing. So much for martyrs. We have erected a wall of separation, not between church and state, but between faith and public life. Thus Christ's teachings about money and power are gently and graciously ignored when real power and good money are at stake. His teachings about forgiveness and love dissolve away when we are confronted with a real enemy. His warnings about priestly privilege somehow do not apply to us priests. His concern for the alien and homeless is presumed to be directed to some other group than our undeserving poor.

The robust implications of faith are pocketed away for private examination but not public display. We don't want to cause trouble for the world's business as usual.

Stephen's bold challenge to the world around him is matched by his intrepid personal reliance on Christ. Thus, even as he is being stoned to death he prays with confidence, "Lord Jesus, receive my spirit." He is unafraid to face the challenges of the earth; he is fearless before the stare of death. And his last words are an equally bold request, that his death not be held against his killers. A book of revelation in himself, Stephen ends it all with "Amen! Come, Lord Jesus!"

Is this what the young Saul saw in the martyrdom he observed? Was it the daring proclamation or the even more daring trust? Might this have been the bloodshed that became a seed of faith?

Stephen, like all martyrs, took seriously Jesus' priestly prayer in the fourth Gospel. Jesus asked that others would believe in him through his disciples' words of life and deeds of love. He wanted the world to know that he was sent for a reason. His martyrs believed it.

31. The Difference It Makes

Acts 2:1–11; 1 Cor. 12:3–7, 12–13; Jn. 20:19–23

"As the Father sent me, so I send you."

Does being a Christian make any difference? Being a Catholic? On Pentecost we are supposed to celebrate the church, but what is the church? It is expected that we cherish our faith, that we value it enough to pass it on. But is it worth it? Is our church really all that much a cause for celebration? Has our faith been worth receiving? Is it worth giving?

These days, I guess, we are not supposed to be too proud of our traditions and our identity. After all, diversity is king. One faith, we are told, is as good as another. There are many paths to the mountain top. Why should we be so arrogant as to assume that ours is the best?

But if we believe that, why would it make much sense to want to proclaim it to anyone else? In fact, if our faith is not all that special, why should we even be grateful for having it? If we have nothing wonderful to give to the world, why would our children want to possess it? If we are so pluralistic as to think that any way to God suffices, why should the way of the Lord Jesus be considered a gift to our young?

It is no secret that many of us elders wonder why so many of our youth seem not to take our church as seriously as we once did (or as seriously as we think we once did). We can say that the homilies are boring, that we should be as entertaining as MTV or the new supermarket cathedrals. We can blame the music, the irritating improvisations, the lack of reverence, the loss of chant, the irrelevance of sermons, the carping about money, the exclusive language, the inclusive language, and an almost infinite number of deficits. But whatever it is, we lack the fire.

It was fire that the Spirit bequeathed to our ancient brothers and sisters. They were so much on fire, they wanted to proclaim it to the world. They spoke of something that made a difference in their lives, something or someone they loved. St. Paul tells us that the something they experienced was enough to make them feel like one vibrant body, unified in a common good and goal. They cherished differences, but only because of the different ways they revealed the one splendor of the gift they shared.

So what is our something, the common gift we share as Catholics? Certainly it is the gift held in common with all Christians: our Gospels, our Lord, our one faith, baptism, and communion. But for Catholics it is more.

The "catholic" dimension is holistic, organic, and integral. We come from a people whose encounter with Jesus Christ is inclusive and capacious. He may speak different tongues to us, but the same truth. He shines in different gifts, but as one giver. He is our one body, our unity, but he thrives through different members. Thus, Catholicism resists any move that reduces Christ to only one facet or moment of experience.

We find him in the holy word. But we know this is a scripture given to us by a community, our community. We see him in community, but we know our community was born of Christ and our memory of him. We pass the word on, but it is the word that made us who we are and brought us together.

As a people, we meet Christ in structures of law, magisterium, and tradition. We see him in those shining lights we call our saints, those leaders we call our hierarchy, those scholars we call our theologians.

We encounter him in the passages of our lives: our birthing and maturing, our failing and healing, our commitments and loves, our feeding and our dying. Thus sacraments, bestowed by Christ and sustained by the church, are signs of his presence holding together the warp and weft of our lives.

We find him in the movements of our hearts: our great pieties and devotions that remind us of the mysteries of his life. We find him in the discernment of spirits, the weighing of forces for joy and sadness. We hear him in the cry of the poor and read him in the signs of the times.

Christ is not confined to any one of these. He is not in our sanctuaries alone. He is not in the law alone. He is not in sacraments alone. He is not in scripture alone. He is not in the magisterium alone. He is not in our devotions, our saints, or our poor alone. He lives in and through them all. And through them all he blesses and calls us. No one of them is supreme. Only he is supreme. And only in him do we find the spirit of God that vivifies all his parts. Such a faith, ultimately faith in a person, deserves our zeal as much as our consent.

I once asked a group of university students if they thought their faith was worth sharing, even preaching to others? The wisest answer was this: If you love someone or something enough, you want to share it. If you are in love, you can't wait to tell someone else. If you love what it means to be a Catholic, it makes all the difference in the world that you give this gift to the ones you love.

Ah, but do we love our faith enough? And do we love the world enough to impart our faith to it?

TRINITY SUNDAY

32. In the Beginning Was Relationship

Prov. 8:22–31; Rom. 5:1–5; Jn. 16:12–15

"Delighting in the human race."

Illusions of autonomy and independence die slowly. We imagine the self as a starting point, a center from which we proceed out to the world. "I think, and so I am," thought Descartes. Thus, he built a philosophical edifice on that clear and distinct foundation, unshaken by doubt. Kant, that other sure modern, tried to save faith as well as science by proposing that the solitary mind could construct both the life of ethics and the world of things. Imperial reason rules reality, and the isolated logic of moral consciousness legislates good and evil.

High ideas, indeed. But the autonomous consciousness of philosophers also haunts the pretensions of everyday life. We are madly in love with individual choice. We decree what is right and wrong; we mouth litanies of our precious individuality: my body, my private property, my rights, my needs, my fulfillment, my conscience, my interests.

Others are the problem. It is they who impinge on our self-determination. They make demands. They want their way. Their sovereign liberty intrudes on ours.

This nagging interference of others, constantly challenging the ego's independent autonomy, led Jean-Paul Sartre to conclude that we do not need the threat of fire and red-hot pokers: "Hell is other people." Otherness is the enemy.

Yet otherness, we remember on Trinity Sunday, is at the very beginning and end of things. Heaven is found in the other.

Wisdom, personified in the Book of Proverbs, speaks: "The Lord begot me, the first-born of his ways, the forerunner of his prodigies. . . ." Before the formation of skies, earth, and sea, "I was beside him as his craftsman, his delight by day, playing all the while." In the beginning was community, otherness of persons within the oneness of God. Existence is not the result of a monad. It is the fruit of mutuality.

In the beginning was the relation of persons: Father, Son, and Spirit, so goes the Trinitarian formula. Yet this "glory be" of mutuality is very different from some contemporary reformulations. Notice how "Creator, Sanctifier, and Redeemer"—a phrase sometimes used today—portrays the Trinity only in terms of its function with respect to the created world. It misses the point that God's actual being is relational. There is otherness in God's oneness. God is the beholder and the beheld, the lover and beloved.

The uncreated Trinity, we Christians believe, is "othered" into creation. Eternal relationship is expressed in space and time. And the created world, thought and loved into being, is empowered to reciprocate. The human creation—"let us create man in our own image and likeness, God said: male and female God created them"—can love the creator back. With faith and hope in the otherness of God, we mirror the personal mutuality of the Trinity and reaffirm the order of all reality.

"And this hope will not leave us disappointed, because the love of God has been poured out in our hearts through the Holy Spirit who has been given to us."

The intimacy which Christ offers us in the fourth Gospel's priestly prayer is the intimacy of persons-in-God.

BODY AND BLOOD OF CHRIST

33. In the Beginning Was Covenant

Gen. 14:18–20; 1 Cor. 11:23–26; Lk. 9:11–17

"Do this in remembrance."

God willed not only to create the world, but to enter into relationship with it. God wanted the created world to be charged with personal existence. Creation would know God back. Creation would love God in return.

And so it was that we were enfranchised with intellect and will, gifts that made possible a free act of love. We were endowed with the ability to commit ourselves. We could enter covenant.

God said, "Let it be." Even more, God said, "I enter into covenant with you." Yet we mere humans were unequal to the task. The risk of personal relationship, of faith and hope and love, while so godly, was somehow also too frightening for us.

It required that we accept our creaturely state. It meant that we would have to admit our dependence upon and our free obedience to the holy other. This, we resisted. And the sorry tale has been told since Eden.

But God was relentless. Even if we reject the proposition, God would ply us with promises of gifts, holy signs, and steadfast guidance. Covenantal relationship, the very life of the Trinity, would never be withdrawn from us, even if we are lost in a sinful state. The divinity would hold itself bound to us. Thus Noah had his rainbow, Abraham his improbable descendants, Moses the covenant of law, David the ark in his palace. And among the prophets of covenant appeared Melchizedek with bread, wine, and blessing given to Abram and Abram's God.

Melchizedek's gesture foreshadowed our final covenant, our new law, our ultimate promise that we make present in Eucharist. Christ's body and blood is the covenant. He himself is the promise of God. We in turn affirm our side of the covenant, proclaiming the mystery of faith: "When we eat this bread and drink this cup, we proclaim your death, Lord Jesus, until you come in glory."

Paul reminded the Corinthians of this covenantal promise in words similar to those we find in Luke and Mark: "This is my body, which is for you. . . . This cup is the new covenant in my blood. . . . Do this in remembrance of me."

Eucharistic images, such as the miraculous multiplication account in the Gospel of Luke, are all harbingers of the undying relationship between God and us. Our daily consecrations remember and re-enact the reality of God's covenantal love.

They also remind us, however, what it is that God so much wants from us. It is that relationship, that free "yes," that gaze back that says with all one's heart, "I do believe, I hope, I love."

The poet Charles Péguy wrote in his work *God Speaks* that after all the magnificence of mountains and depth of the seas, God wanted something else. It was not power or might; it was not the submission of slaves; it was not the automatic response of robots. It was covenant. It was consent. After one has been loved freely in return, submission loses its taste. All the blind submission in the world is not equal to the beautiful soaring-up point in a single invocation of a love that is free.

34. The Gift We Give

Zech. 12:10–11; Gal. 3:26–29; Lk. 9:18–24

"But you: who do you say that I am?"

Peter's profession of faith—"You are the Christ of God"—has often been examined in terms of his own vocation: his calling, his primacy among the apostles, his later failure, and his loving encounter with the Risen Lord.

Considerable attention has also been given to the texts following this event: the first prophecy of Jesus' Passion and the costs of our own discipleship in following him.

What is less often investigated is the reality presumed by Jesus' question. His words reveal something startling about God. They also reveal something wondrous about us.

"But *you*. Who do *you* say that I am?" This, much more than the opinions of the crowd, is Jesus' central interest. He is pre-eminently concerned with the judgment and affirmation of the individual person standing before him. Thus, if we take Peter to be a representation of each of us believers, it becomes clear that what Christ wants of us is our own unique affirmation. No one else can offer our act of assent. All of us have our own hearts to give freely away. This is what God seems to cherish most about us.

When Christ asks each of us, "Who do *you* say that I am?" he exposes the extraordinary character of our being. We persons are able to know our own relationship to the world, to possess it, and then to confer it upon others.

We have an awesome capacity to take hold of our own lives and give them away. In this matter, no one can ever take our place. Only we can utter our fundamental word. Only we can speak for ourselves. Thus, in responding to his question, we discover why each of us is irreplaceable and incomparable. At the same time, we discover our unity as persons: all of us humans are equal in the spiritual grant of freedom. The self-gift of a poor, old, broken-down priest is as valuable to God as the affirmation of any nation's leader.

"Who do *you* say I am?" In our response, being Jew, Greek, black or white, slave or free, old or young, male or female is not significant. What is significant is our freedom, that gift which images most fully our godliness.

We imagine that our foremost task in life is somehow to make a difference, to have done something that no one else could possibly have done, to be irreplaceable. But the only difference we really make in this world, the only thing we can do that no one else can do, is take ownership of our lives and give them away.

This we do in our commitments, in our promises. "I give myself to you in faith." "I believe in you." "I entrust myself to you in hope." "I hope in you." "I say 'yes' to you in love." "This is who I say you are."

Each of these unforced commitments is strangely an empty-ing out, a giving away, a bestowal we make. But in them we discover, too, who and what we are. We find ourselves only when we learn to love, to believe, to hope. We achieve our being only when we no longer cling to it.

"Whosoever of you would cling to your life, will lose it; whosoever lets go of it for my sake will save it."

35. Holy Commitment

1 Kgs. 19:16, 19–21; Gal. 5:13–18; Lk. 9:51–62

"It was for liberty Christ freed us."

Everything else paled when Elisha was anointed by Elijah. He left all for the call. The commitment became his life. The promise was all he would keep of himself.

We do not easily make commitments. Still less easily do we keep them. This is true of any time and nation. And yet it is particularly true of us. These days, it is difficult for a person to keep a promise fifty hours, much less fifty years.

And so we avoid commitments or postpone promises. "I will be your follower wherever you may go." But it will have to wait. I have other things to do, jobs to accomplish, plans to realize. "Let me bury my father first. . . . Let me return to what I cherish." I am not ready to give it all away.

It is often presumed that freedom is a state of being loose and unattached. Some people go so far as to think they lose their freedom when they commit themselves. Freedom is construed as giving in to any immediate desire and impulse. And yet such a notion of freedom—"giving free rein to the flesh," Paul calls it—is slavery. We only begin to be free when we start the process of self-definition called commitment. And our freedom is only realized when we give ourselves away in love. Our commitments, ultimately, are our homeland, our nests, our lairs. They are where we reside, where we center our being.

Such a prospect is awesome: that our fundamental task and responsibility is to commit in love. This is why, like the Galatians, we might be frightened by such liberty. Comfort and escape, as well as other cravings of the flesh, entice us when we confront freedom's awesome implications.

Viktor Frankl, in *The Doctor and the Soul*, wrote of the stakes involved when we face our true liberty: "As soon as we lend our minds to the essence of human responsibility, we cannot forbear to shudder: there is something fearful about human responsibility. But at the same time something glorious. . . . It is glorious to know that the future of the things and the people around us is dependent—even if only to a tiny extent—upon our decision at any given moment. What we actualize by that decision, what we thereby bring into the world, is saved; we have conferred reality upon it and preserved it from passing."

Perhaps the only lasting things we humans make in this world are our promises, our commitments. Perhaps, too, our promises are the only parts of us that we ultimately keep. Without such making and keeping, it could be possible that we die having never fully lived. But when we make bold to respond to the vocation of our humanity, that call to loving commitment given us by God and nurtured by Christ's Spirit, we partake in the very life of our Creator.

"It was for liberty that Christ freed us. So stand firm, and do not take upon yourselves the yoke of slavery a second time."

36. Blessed Assurance

Is. 66:10–14; Gal. 6:14–18; Lk. 10:1–9

"You shall be carried in her arms."

The first Pope John Paul, that smiling priest who reigned only a few weeks, reminded us that God is not only a father, but a mother as well. Was he influenced by the words of Isaiah, "As a mother comforts her child, so will I comfort you"?

The image suggests a privileged intimacy, a wondrous dependency, even a child's first ecstasy. Have you ever seen a nursing babe, arms outstretched and lost in speechless delight? Is that what Isaiah was getting at? Is that how God is to us?

Though we live in a time when some mothers abandon children or even end their lives for some ungodly reason, there is something deep in us that says, if we cannot trust a mother's love, what else is there we might trust?

If the God we worship is imaged in a mother's love, how could we ever fear peril? How could our deepest heart's desires not be met? Even in the midst of threats or most painful relinquishments, we need not worry. The love that holds us close is the final act.

Since the cross of Christ reveals God's undying bond with us, Paul can voice a fearless proclamation to the Galatians: "May I never boast of anything but the cross of our Lord Jesus Christ. Through it, the world has been crucified to me and I to the world." He is utterly rooted in trust, the blessed assurance in a God who bears and nourishes us, who wants only our life and flourishing, who would die for love of us. If we believe this rule of life, we find peace and mercy. "Henceforth let no one trouble me, for I bear the brand marks of Jesus on my body."

Yet troubled we are in this life's sojourn. We hoard a stash of securities. Maybe they will be our insurance policy, our steadfast guards and providers. Worse, even ordinary journeys stir fears of insecurity. Any long walk, to say nothing of the walk of a lifetime, calls for baggage.

On my last long journey, to Africa, I hauled along antibiotics, muscle relaxants lest my back go out, hydrocortisone, Cutters lotion to keep the mosquitoes from my skin, and a net to keep them at an even greater distance. I brought books to ground me, mementoes to tell me who I was. I lugged a special pair of shoes, a raincoat to meet unplanned events. I almost bore my own hypodermics, lest my skin be pricked by some unsterilized invader.

How unlike the Seventy-two I was: they set out to every town as lambs among the wolves, I an immunized calculator of risks. I carried not just a walking staff, but extra luggage for the change of seasons; not just a traveling bag, but boxes of insurance; not just sandals, but a reversible raincoat. I carried much more than the peace of Luke's Gospel. In fact, having so much else, perhaps I never took time to bestow peace.

So I wonder. Who will truly harvest the mystery of our redemption? Will it be the likes of me, so prone to place my trust in trinkets rather than my God? Or will it be a traveler so light and unburdened that all around imagine nothing more wondrous to rely on than a God who would carry us in her arms and fondle us in her lap. "As a mother comforts her child, so I will comfort you."

37. Freedom on the Journey

Dt. 30:10–14; Col. 1:15–20; Lk. 10:25–37

"What must I do?"

The restless heart murmurs: "If only I knew the will of God. If it were only clear what was wanted of me, I would be willing to do it. But things are so complex, and God's will is difficult to discern."

Yet Moses said that God's voice rings loud and bright, signaling our return to him, if only we heed it and give it our allegiance. God's will is not opaque and distant. If we listen, it sounds within us. "For this command which I enjoin on you today is not too mysterious and remote for you. It is not up in the sky. No, it is something very near to you, already in your mouths and in your hearts; you have only to carry it out."

There are times when it all seems clear. The heart moves. We know in our bones what must be done. Like the lawyer, we see the law so simply drawn: "You shall love the Lord your God with all your heart, with all your soul, with all your strength, and with all your mind, and your neighbor as yourself."

Ah, but the living of it, that is the problem. "You have only to carry it out," to will the act, to do it. There's the rub.

Even after hearing the story of the Good Samaritan, we balk and repeat the question: Who, indeed, is our neighbor? Surely not the people in our streets. Surely not the poor of the world. Surely not this particular person here and now before me.

And there are many reasons not to stop. I may get sued. Others will come to help. I'm in a hurry. The poor wretch should have planned for disaster. Charity begins at home.

How well I know the excuses, myself a teacher and priest. It was such as I who passed the broken man on the road to Jericho. And I have done the same.

An armless and legless beggar rolling in a Calcutta gutter could not move me to act. I had things to do. He might be part of a racket (what cost he paid for such a ruse!). He will only want more. Others will expect as much from me. My help will only perpetuate his helpless condition. My pittance will do nothing in the long run.

So I, the priest and teacher, passed him by, trying not to notice. It was not the first time. Nor was it the last.

My seeming inability to be a neighbor is hard to reconcile with my professed desire to follow Christ. The will of God still draws close and clear, nudging my heart. And yet I seem at a loss as to the doing of it. The peace I seek is beyond my reach, exceeding both my virtue and my will.

And in those sadly familiar moments when I inspect the abyss between the holy desires God has placed deep in my soul and the sorry fruit of them, I can only turn to the words of Paul, realizing once again that I will never find peace or reconciliation on my own.

"It pleased God to make absolute fullness reside in him and by means of him to reconcile everything in his person, everything, I say, both on earth and in the heavens, making peace through the blood of the cross."

Do these words, then, absolve me of the struggle? No. But they do remind me that I will never want to approach the throne of Jesus. I—the lawyer—pleading my case. Let the unrest continue, so that, as journeys to Jericho recur in my life, I realize that the only times I will find my neighbor are when I am generous enough to become one.

38. Working and Wanting

Gen. 18:1–10; Col. 1:24–28; Lk. 10:38–42

"Anxious and upset about many things."

The story of Mary and Martha has always irritated me a bit. You have these two sisters. One of them, Martha, takes the opportunity to welcome Jesus into their home. The other, Mary, as soon as Jesus comes in, sits down at his feet and seems to hang on his every word. So what is Martha to do? Sit down too, and let the stew boil over? If she also rests at Jesus' feet, who is going to serve? How will they eat? What will they have? Nothing will get done.

Then Jesus gets on her case, telling her that she frets and bothers about many things and that Mary (of all people) has chosen the better part by just lolling there doing nothing.

I would like to have been a mouse in that house to hear what Martha might have answered. "O.K., you two make the dinner, set out the meal, and clean up the place. I'm tired of working and being unappreciated." Perhaps she would even remind them who had invited Jesus in the first place. At least that is what I would have said, or maybe muttered into the fire that no one else bothered to stoke.

Of course, my perfect riposte reveals why Jesus saw fit to chide the Martha in me. He spots the resentment that rises when I think others are not doing their share—especially when I am so dutifully doing mine. My urgent solicitude reveals something quite other than generosity. So does my reminder that I, after all, am why this little get-together is even happening. Poor me, I brood with perfect logic: If that is the way he wants it, let him have it. "You do the work, if you think it is so paltry."

I finally squeeze into the teeny tight hollow of my ego.

Ah, but there are those other days, those lovely times of labor when I'm not looking over my shoulder at how well I am doing and how little others seem to accomplish. Like Abraham's Sarah with her warm bread, choice meats, and fresh milk, I can go about my tasks knowing that they, too, are the presence of God. My work is no longer something exacted of me, toil grudgingly given. Rather, it flows freely, a display of how good it is to be alive, to be here, to be now.

The Martha in my mind is not distracted on those good days. Nor do I feel any need to complain to God that others around are not following my script. Best of all, I do not complain that I am doing it all by myself.

Those days are rare. But when they arrive I realize that my annoyance with the story of Mary and Martha is not about the value of work, but about the way we work. Martha, like me, need not stop the labor. We just need to stop the fuss.

There is Martha, that saint, in all of us. Just as there is Mary, a saint as well. In fact, there is probably a lot of Mary in Martha and a lot of Martha in Mary. The challenge is in letting them get along. And when we sit down before the feet of God, let not our Martha fail to rejoice in the moment. And when we go about preparing the meals of life, let us labor, not with comparisons or resentment, but with the joy of having seized an opportune moment.

Seventeenth Sunday in Ordinary Time

39. Praying and Pleading

Gen. 18:20–32; Col. 2:12–14; Lk. 11:1–13

"The one who asks always receives."

Abraham had better results from his prayer than most of us do in a lifetime. Take the story of Sodom and Gomorrah. God, having heard the outcry against these two towns whose sins were great and grave, was ready to destroy them both.

Appealing to God's better instincts, Abraham plea-bargains: "Will you sweep away the innocent with the guilty? Suppose there were fifty innocent people in the city; would you wipe out the place?" Then the clincher: "Far be it from you to do such a thing."

It worked! Not only once, but five times. In answer to Abraham's petition, God was willing to preserve the towns for a mere ten innocent people.

But as we know from the rest of this sad tale, there weren't even ten to be found. And although Lot and his family were spared, Sodom and Gomorrah were destroyed.

I heard this story as a young child, first wondrously recounted by my aunt, a Sister of Saint Joseph, and then later in Bible history class. I remember thinking: "Go, Abraham, go. Ask God for five." Ever since, I've had strong tendencies to be a bargainer, maybe even a canon lawyer, and certainly a petitioner.

I ask God for everything I want but am nowhere near as successful as Abraham. I ask for health, miracles, X-ray vision to find lost articles, and, interminably, to be a better person.

Why not? Jesus said we should pray for our daily bread. That covers a lot. How many times, late at night, have I pounded on the door of heaven, remembering his words from

Luke's Gospel: "Ask and you shall receive, seek and you shall find, knock and it shall be opened to you."

I have asked and sought and knocked so much, you'd think I would know better by now.

Either the problem is with me or it is with God: take your choice. For myself, as the years go on, I think the problem is mine—or at least what I ask for and why I ask.

Behind most of my prayers is a gnawing fear of losing the loves of this life, so ephemeral and bittersweet. Although most of the things I ask for are by and large good, I have come to think that my desire to secure them suffers from a paradoxical dilemma. In all my pleas, especially for what I love most, I am really asking that they never die, that they never be lost irreparably. But clearly, if nothing we love could ever die to this world, we would all end up decrepit bags of bones on a depleted earth. In fact, we would have to be made of non-biodegradable plastic; but then how could we love, much less grow? That cannot be the answer.

Perhaps this is. Jesus teaches us to pray to our God as a father in heaven. And his promise is that, beyond this earth, none of its goods we cherish will ever be stolen away.

"What parent among you will give your child a snake if he asks for a fish, or hand her a scorpion if she asks for an egg? If you, with all your sins, know how to give your children good things, how much more will the heavenly Father give the Holy Spirit to those who ask him."

40. The High and Holy Realm

Ec. 1:2, 2:21–23; Col. 3:1–5, 9–11; Lk. 12:13–21

Dan. 7:9-10, 13-14; 2 Pt. 1:16-19; Mt. 17:1-9

"A lamp shining in a dark place."

"I've been to the mountaintop," Martin Luther King, Jr., said shortly before his murder. From there, on the privileged heights, he saw the promised land of great transformations—another way, another hope, another kingdom. It was not the shadowy world of night's clashing armies, but of the bright dawn of justice and peace.

The mountain is the place of visions. There we find a lookout over distant realms. The mountain manifests beatitudes, eternal covenants, solitary confrontation with the most holy and high.

It was on the mountain that Jesus became transfigured before his apostles' eyes, his human and familiar face now dazzling as the sun, the ordinary clothes shimmering in light. He was in conversation with the great ones, Moses and Elijah; and out of clouds came the voice: "This is my beloved son on whom my favor rests. Listen to him."

Listen to him. Christ is a message sent to us from afar, the Second Letter of Peter says, prophetic and reliable, a unique word from another world, not something fabricated by human imagination or earthly construct. As the prophet Daniel dreamed, the mountain of transfiguration became the throne of the promised one, who, before the voice of heaven, would receive "dominion, glory and kingship. Nations and peoples of every language serve him. His dominion is an everlasting dominion that shall not be taken away; his kingship shall not be destroyed."

On the mountain, our attention searches out the promise that shines over dark places, the first streak of dawn, the rising morning star in our hearts. The mountain is our Sinai, bearing our new Moses, our new law, which has the human name of Jesus. It is our own Horeb, upon which walks the final prophet, so much greater than Elijah.

Let us make no mistake about it. In these days, when voices advise us to entertain other, more pliable gods and goddesses, we must decide to whom we will listen. Who will win our attention and allegiance?

Will we be held in thrall by smoldering spirits of the earth and its murmurs? Will we acquiesce to the lords of culture and those who manicure our surface image? Will we obey the blind and uncaring laws of planetary mechanics? Will we believe the pimps of ego who assure us we need listen to nothing other than our impulse? Will we cling to cleverly concocted myth?

The readings for the eighteenth Sunday in Ordinary Time are warnings about the illusions that beset us, the sounds of the sirens that lure us. The anxiety and toil of Ecclesiastes, the idolatry and obsessions mentioned in Colossians, the voracious greed portrayed in the gospel parable all clamor for our attention.

But the transfiguration scene reminds us that, as followers of Christ, a different voice sounds in our hearts. It is the voice of the High and Holy One, spoken from afar, but given human resonance. "This, this one is my beloved."

Ours is a plain and crucial choice. On the mountain of transfiguration is the holy ground of recommitment.

Who will be our God? Before what powers will we fall on our knees? If we go to the mountain of the beloved and listen to him, he will call forth our slumbering powers. "Get up. Do not be afraid." And when we rise to our feet, looking up and out, ready to descend the heights, may our eyes fall upon no one else but only Jesus.

41. Ancestral Courage

Wis. 18:6–9; Heb. 11:1–2, 8–19; Lk. 12:32–48

"A cloud of witnesses."

What is faith? The writer of the Letter to the Hebrews tells us: "Faith is confident assurance concerning what we hope for, and conviction about things we do not see." It is not a function of organic vision. Rather, it is an act of seeing in trust.

Long ago, when I spent a month working at the "house of the dying" in Calcutta, I sought a sure answer to my future. On the first morning I met Mother Teresa after Mass at dawn. She asked, "And what can I do for you?" I asked her to pray for me. "What do you want me to pray for?" I voiced the request I had borne thousands of miles: "Pray that I have clarity."

She said no. That was that. When I asked why, she announced that clarity was the last thing I was clinging to and had to let go of. When I commented that she herself had always seemed to have the clarity I longed for, she laughed: "I have never had clarity; what I've always had is trust. So I will pray that you trust."

Thus Mother Teresa became for me a member of that cloud of witnesses to which the Letter to the Hebrews refers: heroes of faith, who had conviction about things unseen. So it was with Abraham and Sarah, who believed they would give birth to a child in their old age (the very idea was enough to make Sarah laugh out loud) and make "descendants as numerous as the stars in the sky and the sands of the seashore."

The Letter to the Hebrews celebrates the faith of Abel, dead but still teaching us; of Noah and his improbable ark; of Jacob, at death's door, finally able to bless Joseph's sons; of Moses, the child unguarded and abandoned, who would one day lead

a nation, against impossible odds, into a territory his feet
would never touch. Faith felled the walls of Jericho and saved
the prostitute Rahab. It was faith, the letter says, that discov-
ered new lands, bestowed wondrous strength, and inspired
uncommon courage in ordinary men and women. "Some were
pilloried, flogged, even chained in prison, stoned, beheaded,
homeless, dressed in rags, penniless, given nothing but ill-
treatment, living in caves and deserts and ravines." They were
all heroes of faith, the letter continues, but they did not live to
see what was promised.

How much we have to learn from the great ones who have
gone before us, not only the Hebrew saints praised above, but
our own as well—those who, after Christ, believed in him
despite adversity.

We imagine faith to ease confusion, dull the pain, redeem
the times, but we miss the testimony of the clouds of witnesses.
Our faith does not bring final clarity on this earth. It does not
disarm the demons. It does not still the chaos or dull the pain
or provide a crutch so we might walk. When all else is unclear,
the heart of faith says, "Into your hands I commend my spirit."

So it was with all our heroes. "These died in faith. They did
not obtain what had been promised but saw and saluted it
from afar . . . searching for a better, a heavenly home."

42. Disturbing Faith

Jer. 38:4–6, 8–10; Heb. 12:1–4; Lk. 12:49–53

"How I wish the blaze were ignited."

I once received a letter from a young seminarian who told of
his desire to live the gospel wholeheartedly. The main barrier,
he confessed, was the advice from a few elders warning him

that he should not get carried away. It reminded me of the time when, as a young Jesuit, I read the Gospels seriously for the first time. There was a passion and intensity to them that could set one on fire. What a powerful vision, what a wondrous revolution the Gospels heralded.

I, too, heard the advice of prudent minds. "Don't get carried away. We don't want you going off the deep end." That was only the first time I received counsel which, though offered in charity, seemed to tame something unleashed in me whenever I read the Gospels. After all, one did not want to burn out, much less cause trouble.

But that's what the Gospels do. They start fires in us. They cause trouble. The Gospels are a pain in the neck of prudent heads and moderate minds. They are surely a greater threat to worldly or church authority than Jeremiah was to those princes who wanted him put to death for demoralizing the army and people. They threw Jeremiah in a cistern, where he became the proverbial "stick-in-the-mud." Jesus we just stick on a wall. We paint him pious, nice, and pretty, surely not a troublemaker or a firebrand.

Or was he? "I have come to light a fire on the earth. How I wish the blaze were ignited. . . . Do you think I have come to establish peace on the earth? The contrary is true; I have come for division."

Now, of course, we know that this is not the whole story. After all, he was called the Prince of Peace, and he promised a peace that "the world cannot give." As for causing division, why would his priestly prayer ask that we might be completely one in him and each other? Moreover, the Gospels readily provide a litany of love. The problem is, I believe, that the love and unity Christ offers are at odds with the counterfeits we coin. If Christ's peace takes hold of us, it brings an interior freedom that makes us dangerous and divisive, especially if we cannot be bought off or intimidated.

His unity is repugnant to any person or culture that demands moral accommodation as its cost. His love is obnoxious to anyone who thinks charity begins at home. His peace does not come cheap. In fact, in this matter of following Christ, even households can be divided if the price of unity is deception. Brothers and sisters, whether in blood or in community of faith, can find themselves in opposition.

The command of love stokes the fire of conflict—both with others and within our hearts—over money, territory, family, and tribe. Love in itself, much more strong and abiding than a spark of quick passion, is a refining blaze of covenant and fidelity.

Peace and unity will come, not by dousing the fire of faith or declaring a false truce with evil, but by focusing our attention on the one who kindled love in the first place. "Let us keep our eyes fixed on Jesus, who inspires. . . . Remember him. Do not grow despondent or abandon the struggle."

43. Consoling Hope

Is. 66:18–21; Heb. 12:5–7, 11–13; Lk. 13:22–30

"Steady your trembling knees."

I know a good and graced woman, now in her eighties, who sometimes seems a bit queasy about the aftermath of her death. She said one day, "I hope I don't die in my sleep; I'm not sure I'll like where I wake up." I may be wrong, but I detected an apprehension in her, not unlike that of other virtuous people who wonder about their eternal fate.

Most young people are said to believe in a hell where nobody goes. Many others, perhaps adults, think there is a hell largely populated by enemies. And among the old are believers who nervously wonder if hell might be populated by the likes of themselves. They, like St. Paul at some moments, consider the question of their salvation "in fear and trembling."

They may have good reason. When someone asked Jesus whether a small number would be saved, he was not very comforting: "Try to come in through the narrow door. Many, I tell you, will try to enter and be unable." The lord of the household seems not to acknowledge those standing outside, knocking and pleading for entry, even though they had once been in his company. What is more, there will be that horrible "wailing and grinding of teeth" by those rejected.

If this is the discipline that the Letter to the Hebrews refers to, it is difficult, despite the advice, not to lose heart. After all, what comfort is there in the prospect that we might not be saved or accepted into Christ's heavenly kingdom?

The allusion to the narrow gate is found in Luke's thirteenth chapter, which contrasts a self-defeating hardness of heart with redemptive repentance. Those whose faith is sterile and lifeless hurt only themselves. Those who are hypocrites fix their fate when they reject the truth. Those who, with Herod, hate Jesus slam the door on their salvation. And those who refuse to be gathered in by him as chicks are gathered by their mother are left to their own scattered journey.

The narrow gates of the old cities were wide enough for a person to get through. It is the size of a person because it is a person. Jesus is the narrow gate, the way by which any person can get through to the heavenly city.

In all the debates over who and how many will be saved, in our own wonderings about our own eternal lot, it is instructive to remember a truth that is disconcerting yet calming. We all most likely deserve a fate far less glorious than heaven. After all, would not all of us be lost without him? But through him, the narrow gate, all may enter paradise, one by one in salvation's long procession.

We do not know for sure; but perhaps there was a generous wisdom far greater than we realized in that old prayer often said amid the rosary mysteries of our redeemer's life.

"Dear Jesus, save us from the fires of hell. Bring all souls to heaven, especially those most in need of your mercy."

That is a prayer to the narrow gate, wide enough, however, for all to enter, even those who die in their sleep.

Twenty-second Sunday in Ordinary Time

44. Reversals of Fortune

Sir. 3:17–20, 28–29; Heb. 12:18–19, 22–24;
Lk. 14:1, 7–14

"Some who are first will be last."

One tradition in the Hebrew scriptures, especially in the wisdom literature, frequently highlights the irony of inverted expectations. Thus, Sirach's sage teaches that love is experienced in giving, rather than receiving; that greatness is revealed in humility; that wisdom is a better listener than talker. The Psalms tell us that God becomes the dwelling of the homeless, the liberty of prisoners, and refreshing rain for dry hearts.

The Letter to the Hebrews has the same tinge of paradox. While many might think God is as unapproachable as the highest mountain, or an all-consuming furnace of rage, or an abyss of impenetrable darkness, or a booming voice so terrible one might wish it had never been heard, the God of the Letter to the Hebrews is a loving parent. God's mountain is Zion, full of life, bright with light, ringing with festivity. God's sound is the voice of Jesus, through whom our maimed limbs will become whole again.

Luke's Jesus is fully a child of this oral tradition of paradoxical reversals. His own wisdom teaching, offered at a banquet of elite lawyers and pharisees, actually draws upon the advice in Proverbs (25:7) that it is "better to be invited, 'Come up here,' than be humiliated in the presence of the prince."

Jesus' own parable portrays people seeking the place of honor who are eventually asked to move, now blushing, to a lower place. "What you should do when you have been invited is go and sit in the lowest place, so that when your host approaches you he will say, 'My friend, come up higher.'"

This seems like a bit of advice from Dale Carnegie on how to win friends and influence people: If you want to look good, put on the mask of humility. But it is clear that Jesus is not offering mere courtly etiquette. He is talking about an existential reality. Those who exalt themselves, whether covertly or openly, will be humbled, and all who humble themselves shall be exalted.

It is not only guests who have the problem of ego-enhancement. The host does too. Elite house parties, whether hosted in Greek and Roman times or our own day, are honored by the best and brightest who attend. Such worldly wisdom is reversed as well. It is better, Jesus says, that we invite the unwanted and discarded to our dinners and be happy when they cannot repay us. For our payment will be in heaven.

This poses a still deeper paradox. Is Jesus suggesting that we act humbly only for the reason that we might be exalted? Is he advising us to use the poor as our stepping stone to heaven's highest places?

I think not. Jesus is speaking to a group of people who set traps to catch him, who seem to understand only the logic of self-enhancement. Even on their own terms, their tactics are self-defeating. No matter what tactic of self-promotion they try, they will fail.

Pretending to be the least will not yield greatness in the kingdom of heaven. Luke is not presenting a stratagem to win approval. He is describing again something already expressed by Mary herself, that God routs the proud of heart, dethrones the worldly prince, and exalts the lowly. In such matters, faking it will not do the trick.

45. Eternal Vigilance

Wis. 9:13–18; Phlm. 9–10, 12–17; Lk. 14:25–33

"What is within our grasp, we find with difficulty."

Long ago—it seems as if in another world—I took part in a televised debate over military expenditures and nuclear bombs. The woman I faced was such a good debater that the producer of the program called me three times beforehand to make sure I knew what I was getting into. He seemed amazed that I was still willing to go through with it.

She drew blood. Her most wounding thrust was scripture-based. "Jesus himself," she said, "told us, 'If a king is about to march on another king to do battle, will he not sit down first and consider whether, with ten thousand men, he can withstand an enemy coming at him with twenty thousand? If he cannot, he will send a delegation while the enemy is at a distance, asking for terms of peace.'" I remembered the story from Luke's Gospel, but before I could think of the context, my opponent came at me with the coup de grâce. "It's easy for you to lay down arms and to be a pacifist. You don't have a wife and children to take care of. If you did, you'd thank God for the bomb."

What a sweet paradox it all was. The military analogy from Luke is actually about the vigilance we need for discipleship, especially in letting go of the earthly things that we cling to as our property. That is why Jesus concludes the story with, "In the same way, none of you can be my disciple if you do not renounce all your possessions." It has nothing to do with the evangelical approval of armies. It has everything to do with the dangers in clinging to things and people as our possessions.

Jesus' recommendation of vigilance against possessiveness comes in one of the harshest passages found in the New Testament, a saying about family life. "If any of you comes to me without turning your back on father and mother, spouse and children, brothers and sisters, indeed your very self, you cannot be my follower." We must, rather, take up our cross and follow him in discipleship.

Clearly he is speaking here of renouncing our loved ones as possessions or as barriers to the redeeming cross. We can never possess another. (This is why Paul, in his Letter to Philemon, undercuts slavery by insisting that Onesimus is not a slave, but a loved brother.) What is more, we can never be another's god. Nor can another human serve as ours. No one can save us but Christ.

I cannot speak from direct experience of having spouse or children, but I suspect that there is a great and paradoxical truth in what Jesus says. If we treat our children as if they are either our possessions or our gods, it will not only be impossible to follow Christ; it will be impossible to love them. We will strangle them by clinging to them as if they were our property or crush them with the impossible burden of saving us and making us happy.

"For the deliberations of mortals are timid, and unsure are our plans. . . . Scarce do we guess the things on earth, and what is within our grasp, we find with difficulty."

I may have lost the debate. But I found something else.

46. Prodigal Love

Ex. 32:7–11, 13–15; 1 Tim. 1:12-17; Lk. 15:1-32

"He welcomes sinners."

The first directed retreat I ever gave was a harrowing experience. An older Jesuit had invited me to be on a team that was to direct thirty monks at a secluded monastery. I first begged off, saying I had never given a retreat before. He replied, "With that excuse you'll successfully avoid ever giving one." Then I told him that giving a retreat to holy monks would be like teaching Pavarotti to sing. He didn't think that was very funny, though it did display a little pride masked as humility. Finally I said I was too young. He said that was balderdash.

As it turned out, I was right, at least on the third count. One of my retreatants, so old I'm sure he's now in heaven, announced to me on the fifth day of the retreat that he could never open his soul to me, so young and hippie-looking. What's more, from day one he had been disappointed that he had not been given a more mature religious as director.

What distracted me from my ego's wounds were the marvels of the spiritual lives of these men (including my reluctant retreatant). And still vital, after almost twenty-five years, is the memory of one monk who spent a whole day wrestling with the parable of the prodigal son.

"I've prayed and prayed about this, and I've found out who's really at fault in this story."

I couldn't wait to hear.

"The father! He's the problem. Why didn't he ever tell the good son he was doing a good job? Why didn't he put on a lavish banquet for him? Why did he make such a commotion over a ne'er-do-well who squandered half the fortune and now will probably get another half of what rightly belonged to the first?"

He had a point.

During another retreat, a man with a wife and children once told me, "If you run a family like the father of the prodigal son did, they will walk all over you."

He had a point too.

I'll certainly have a few memories to heal in heaven if I find out that some profligate or oppressor was forgiven and even given a higher place than mine. I gag at the thought that Hitler might be there. And what a surprise if Nietzsche, that inveterate atheist, like a lost and recovered sheep, shows up at the banquet. What will I do if the Marquis de Sade, a bad penny if there ever was one, is found up there like a prized lost coin?

The whole thing is disconcerting. So it must have been to those priests and writers, the pharisees and scribes, who murmured when tax collectors and sinners—of all people—were gathering around to hear Jesus. "This man welcomes sinners and eats with them." Harrumph. Then he regales us with stories of a lost penitent, more celebrated than 99 of us righteous, and a recovered coin more pleasing to the angels than nine coins never lost. As a final insult, Jesus caps off his sermon with the story of that spoiled kid.

If one of my siblings returned from a wild and woolly time, I probably would have sulked and stayed away from the party too. I would have made it quite clear that I was not enjoying the music and dance. And I wonder: Would I also refuse to join the joy, even if my father pleaded with me? Would I listen to his words? "My son, you are with me always, and everything I have is yours."

Would he have to remind me of my own blindness? Of my squandering of life? Of my reluctance to celebrate the good? Of my own sinfulness?

One need not be St. Paul, once a blasphemer, a persecutor, a man filled with arrogance, to thank God for being treated mercifully in this life and hereafter. One need not be as derelict or depraved as Moses' stiff-necked bunch worshiping a molten calf, to appreciate God's forgiveness. High in grace or sunk in sin, we all know the kind of favor Jesus granted in overflowing measure. "You can depend on this as worthy of full acceptance: that Christ Jesus came into the world to save sinners."

Each of us, in little and large ways, ought to be thankful for unmerited love and leave the accounting to God.

There is something good in the worst of us and something bad in the best of us, my own father used to say. He too had a point.

Perhaps that is why repentance is always the start of good news. Perhaps that is why our song of God's glory so aptly follows the confession of our sins.

Glorying in God's loving forgiveness calls forth a third son or daughter in us. This would be the one who, after a life of bright fidelity, generous sacrifice, and courage in the face of great odds, comes to the heavenly banquet and sees a spectrum of other children there. Some of them have had a far easier time of it on earth. Others seem surprised at being there themselves. A few (many? all?) really didn't even deserve to be there. To each God says, "Welcome, dear and precious one; all I have is yours."

Upon being asked whether the rewards are unfair or whether she would have lived her life differently, this third child says, "No. I would do it all over again for such a God, who has such love in such bounty and beauty."

47. Problems with Personal Money

Amos 8:4–7; 1 Tim. 2:1–8; Lk. 16:1–13

"You cannot give yourself to God and money."

Possessions. Investments. Financial security. I find the whole issue painful to face in the Gospels. This strikes some of my friends as ludicrous, since I do not appear to involve myself much with money, living as I do, under the vow of poverty. In fact, we Jesuits take an extra vow concerning poverty that promises, in effect, never to change the vow of poverty except to make it more strict.

Yet our use of money has always haunted us Jesuits, whether in our general or provincial congregations, our rules, our traditions, or our community squabbles. For the most part we live a modest, even simple life. But by the standards of living in most quarters of the earth, we live in uncommon security and abundance. In comparison even with the ordinary parish priest or middle-class family, dogged by bills, taxes, and debt, I live a comfy existence.

As the story goes, a young graduate of a Jesuit university, happening upon one of our community recreation areas with its filled refrigerators, fine furniture, and inviting television rooms, quips, "If this is poverty, show me chastity."

Some members of the Society of Jesus, whether young or old, hidden or famous, do far better than the rest of us in living frugal lives. They can be found in college administrations as well as in the hills of Honduras. But even they have security about education, health care, and lodging that most people in the world can only imagine.

And so for Jesuits, as for many Christians who wish to follow Christ and yet find themselves rich in material things, Gospel teachings concerning money are troubling. At times it becomes so perplexing that we are tempted to stop searching for a solution. This has been true in my own case. It seems so hard, even impossible, to integrate my material security with full discipleship that I often give up trying to figure it out. Maybe it will all go away.

Jesus, in the Gospel according to Luke, tells us that we should not give up the effort. This is the recommendation (not advice to deceive and manipulate) behind the story of the unjust steward. The steward musters every available bit of far-sightedness and craft when it comes to working out his material fate. And he is dealing with mere earthly things. We, however, are trying to figure out something that touches the very meaning of who we are and what we forever cling to.

Luke himself provides two guidelines to help us figure out our relationship to money. The whole of chapter 16, with its four interrelated sections, exemplifies the first guideline: Money is for persons and the only proper use of it is in sharing. What is more, those who make special claim on our sharing are the poor. This is an inescapable conclusion from Luke's teaching. It is a teaching with ancient pedigree, the same doctrine that led Amos to indict those who "trample upon the needy and destroy the poor of the land." And just as Amos said that God would never forget the exploiting of workers for silver, dress, and drink, so also Luke warned of a dire fate for the rich man in the story of Lazarus.

Luke's second guideline is the pithy moral drawn from the story of the steward: "No servant can serve two masters. Either you will hate the one and love the other or be attentive to the one and despise the other. You cannot give yourself to God and money." The more we allow ourselves to be mastered by money, the more we are likely to despise those who remind us of another dominion. We might even resent the very Gospels that challenge our attachment.

Our attitudes to the poor and our attitudes about security are the best indications of our discipleship. For myself, neither guideline has been very reassuring. Even this summer I was taken aback by the feelings of contempt I have for beggars. While waiting to meet my brother and his wife at a corner in Oxford, I was aloof and abrupt whenever I spotted a hand held out by someone who looked lazy, dirty, or irresponsible, or appeared to be in a drug haze.

When Tom and Maureen came along and quietly gave a few coins to the very people who rankled me, I saw a shadowy glimpse of the truth I had repressed. They were not solving poverty in the world; they were not even solving the imme- diate problem of one person along the sidewalk. They were just reaching out to another human, surely broken and less blessed, and sharing something of what they had.

My brother and his wife, perhaps unwittingly, were remind- ing me of something far more significant than the transitory shame I felt for my smallness. It was once again the call of the Gospels, nudging me not to give up on the poor or the ways, however small and passing, I might give to them.

Twenty-sixth Sunday in Ordinary Time

48. Problems with Corporate Wealth

Amos 6:1, 4–7; 1 Tim. 6:11–16; Lk. 16:19–31

"The love of money is the root of all evils."

What is the "Great Abyss" between Lazarus in the bosom of Abraham and Dives in the bed of flames? What events caused the chasm?

The story Jesus told the Pharisees is well known. A rich person, traditionally called Dives (from the Latin word for "rich"), having lived in opulence all his earthly days, made for himself a destiny of torment. The beggar Lazarus, having longed for the scraps of the rich, his sores licked by dogs, finds consolation. When Dives pleads that further warning be given his brothers, Abraham says only: "If they do not listen to Moses and the prophets, they will not be convinced even if one should rise from the dead."

The chasm is of their own making. The Diveses of the world refuse to listen to the revelations of God, just as they refuse to hear the cry of the poor. Wealth and privilege have created an unbridgeable gap. They just do not need God. They certainly do not need the poor.

And we, this Judeo-Christian nation, who have read Moses' law, who have heard the prophets, and received the good news of Jesus—what might this parable say to us? Have we created an abyss between ourselves and the Lazaruses of the world? Are we guilty of the crimes that Amos attributed to his own people: self-indulgence, frivolous distraction, willful ignorance, and cruel neglect of the poor?

Do we not close our minds to anything that challenges our way of life? We hate to be reminded of the idiocy of our practices: paying $100 million to a convicted rapist for two minutes in a boxing ring, rewarding our entertainers with lavish bounty while resenting the person on welfare, giving golden parachutes to failed C.E.O.'s and nothing to workers laid off as their companies downsize or relocate to more profitable locales. The corporate head of Gap and Banana Republic made a cool $2 million last year. A woman in El Salvador who makes his clothes for us to wear made 56 cents an hour. And now, with our great free market, advertisements in industry trade magazines brag that we can hire seamstresses for 33 cents an hour. U.S. workers are abandoned while Third-World workers are exploited.

Is there something for Amos to chew on here? A prophetic voice of our own time seems to think so and has written about the immoral practices of untrammeled capitalism. But when he defended the primacy of labor in his encyclical *Laborem Exercens* (1981), Pope John Paul II was derided by a columnist in *Fortune* magazine for being "wedded to socialist economics and increasingly a sucker for third world anti-imperialist rhetoric." Even many Catholics, especially the wealthy and powerful, ignore or dismiss the consistent teachings of this pope whenever he talks about money. They see him as a benighted Pole who fails to understand the sanctifying grace of material success.

But John Paul II sees a terrible abyss separating wealth from poverty, a chasm that bodes ill for the poor in this world and for the privileged when they face the next.

It was in North America, at a Mass in Edmonton, Ontario, that the pope's homily on Christ's last judgment reminded us of the fate of Lazarus and Dives: "In the light of Christ's words, the poor South will judge the rich North. And the poor people and poor nations—poor in different ways, not only lacking food, but also deprived of freedom and other human rights—will judge those people who take these goods away from them, amassing to themselves the imperialistic monopoly of economic and political supremacy at the expense of others."

Needless to say, these words were no more welcomed than the Ten Commandments, the prophecy of Amos, and the parables of one who would "rise from the dead."

These interventions from God are not made merely to make us feel guilty. They are meant to empower and free us. If we open our eyes to the Word of God and unstop our ears to hear the cry of the poor, we will not automatically endorse some political or economic policy. But we will insist that any politician or party must welcome and care for Lazarus. We must do this for the sake of Lazarus. We must do it for our own sake.

Paul's First Letter to Timothy reveals the kind of persons we might be: people of integrity, kindness, piety, steadfastness, and love, people who fight the good fight of faith, people of true nobility. This passage in chapter 6, however, is framed by two warnings. It is prefaced by Paul's remark that, if we long to be rich, we will become trapped into dangerous ambitions that plunge us into ruin. The way of Christian nobility, however, is a life of generosity.

> Warn those who are rich in this world's goods that they are not to look down on other people and not to set their hopes on money, which is untrustworthy, but on God, who, out of his riches, gives us all that we need for our happiness. Tell them that they are to do good, and be rich in good works, to be generous and willing to share. This is the way they can save up true capital for the future if they want to make sure of the only life that is real.

I did not dream up that passage to make anyone feel bad. Paul wrote it to help us find joy.

49. Midwives of God

Hab. 1:2–3; 2:2–4; 2 Tim. 1:6–8, 13–14; Lk. 17:5–10

"Strong, loving and wise."

Why is there disorder everywhere? The meanness of discourse. The destruction of life. The sly celebration of evil. The collapse of mercy. The breaking of promises. The pathologies of culture.

With Habakkuk we plead for help, but God seems not to listen. "I cry out to you, 'Violence!' but you do not intervene." There is ruin in our cities, misery for the voiceless old, and skepticism for the hungry young. Wounds abound: Alzheimer's and liver disease, congenital handicaps and ancient vengeances. Even the earth groans with ominous quakes and atmospheric disturbance. Hurricanes follow drought. What is more, we witness within ourselves awesome malevolence. Wars are waged; women are degraded; children are disposed of. We destroy the earth and its species. We uproot and wipe away its peoples. "Destruction and violence are before me; there is strife and discord."

Sometimes it is too much to bear. The scale of the inequity crushes us. The scope of the iniquity, even in one's heart, dwarfs virtue. The good die young. Deceivers prevail. Streets of Manhattan, Hanoi, Johannesburg, and London are lined with empty stares. Automatons move dexterously. There is no eye contact. Politics is posture. The media medicate us. Where is hope? What reasons can be offered to loving spouses that they should bring children into this world? Increase my faith, I say. Give me some reason to believe. Show a sign. Make a promise.

"If you had faith the size of a mustard seed, you could say to this sycamore, 'Be uprooted and transplanted into the sea,' and it would obey you."

Faith. Hope. Love. I have often asked what these paltry human acts might mean to the sweep of history, to the portentous powers of culture, to the lost. How can they give birth to goodness in a world that so often seems to gestate death?

A story I cling to—now recalled from so long ago that I have to ask myself whether memory is true—returns.

There was a religious sister who was a midwife. She taught in a university, and she practiced her profession in a city hospital. Into the hospital walked a lost, young teenager, many months pregnant, not even aware of the fact, but sick.

"I've got news for you," the midwife said. "You're pregnant." There was no boy or man who might claim the name of father, no family, no support group, no promise. As I recall, the young girl did not even know how or when she became pregnant, so meager was her knowledge of "reproductive rights."

The sister-servant promised the young mother-to-be that she would be there for her. Each week a visit could be made and lessons taught: how to eat properly and take care of a pregnant body, how to prepare for delivery, how to live. And each week, visits were made. After the novena of months passed, birth came. One new mother's child, with the midwife's guidance, was fed rightly, nursed and cleaned, cared and worked for.

Then the young mother disappeared. She was gobbled up by this heartless world, lost in the maelstrom of this culture, the American dream, which for her and her child was a nightmare. She went defenseless before the pimps of pleasure and power. She vanished into the dangerous night.

She was not heard from again until, I think, six years later, when in her early twenties she wrote a note to her midwife-mother. It was an invitation, the message now blurred in my mind. "I am sorry I waited so long to thank you, but I wanted to surprise you. I wanted to be like you, since you were someone so good and loving."

The invitation was to a graduation for Licensed Practical Nurses. Somehow, stronger than all the threat of violence and abuse, more appealing than any seduction of the moment, was the gift and promise of a person's witness.

The good is like a frail fire. It expends itself once it is lit, bringing light to those around. Even though slight, it can illuminate a big dark room, helping you make it to the other side. Like love and wisdom, it lives in being communicated, being given.

My midwife-sister-friend did that for a young girl. She did that for me. You just do not know how faith bears fruit. You just do not know how love lives anew.

"I remind you to stir into flame the gift of God bestowed when my hands were laid on you. The Spirit God has given us is no cowardly spirit, but rather one that makes us strong, loving and wise. Therefore, never be ashamed of your testimony to our Lord . . . but with the strength that comes from God, bear your share of hardship which the Gospel entails."

50. Gratitude

2 Kgs. 5:16–17; 2 Tim. 2:8–13; Lk. 17:11–19

"Please accept a gift."

I wonder what happened to the nine lepers who did not go back to thank Jesus. Did their minds immediately turn to other needs, newer preoccupations, more urgent petitions? Did they just move on with their lives, now cured of leprosy but worried about something else? Did they remember how it was when they always kept a distance and ever longed for cleansing?

Maybe, if they had kept a journal of those days, they could have turned back the pages to forgotten times when they cried out for pity or begged for help. They might have remembered how they once thought their whole world would be charged with light if they could be healed, like Naaman, with their skin as fresh as a child's. They could have compared their old feelings about their affliction and their new freedom, having now won their hearts' desire.

There are times when we seem to go through life the way some children go through birthday presents. We tear through the wrapping paper of our gifts, piling up the boxes as we move on to the next bright toy. Perhaps we shake an envelope without reading the message or knowing who it is from. What's next? Is that all?

This perpetual flitting of our interest, this inability to rest in the gift, occurs also in matters of health. We might fret through a night, thinking the heartburn is heart attack, the cold sore is cancer, the next day is treacherous. In a matter of hours, the jeopardy may pass, and we forget the gift as we begin to brood over something else.

So it is with our desires. If only I might be married. If only we might have a child. If only I could change my job.

Often enough the presents arrive. Now married, I long for independence. Now a parent, I await, with hope or alarm, the leave-taking. Now working, I crave for leisure. Now quiet, I am restless for action. Now done with one trial, I expect the next.

Why is it we charge through life so unaware of our million deliverances? Do we appreciate our rescues or healings even a tenth of the time? If we could count the fears, both small or large, that once hounded us, and then thank God for each dreaded outcome never met, we would reach no end to gratitude.

We will not take full possession of our lives until we learn to give thanks for them. We don't really own our legs or eyes, our hands and skin unless we're daily grateful. We don't really live with our loved ones unless we foster an appreciative, almost contemplative sensitivity to their presence. It is only the loss of them— or the threat of it—that shakes us into an awareness of their manifold grace.

But when we wake up from our sleepwalk, when we see the wonder of the smallest parts of our existence, we begin to live. It is then we know what it is like, with the tenth leper, to be saved.

Perhaps the most grateful person I've ever heard of was an old woman in an extended care hospital. She had some kind of wasting disease, her different powers fading away over the march of months. A student of mine happened upon her on a coincidental visit. The student kept going back, drawn by the strange force of the woman's joy. Though she could no longer move her arms and legs, she would say, "I'm just so happy I can move my neck." When she could no longer move her neck, she would say, "I'm just so glad I can hear and see."

When the young student finally asked the old woman what would happen if she lost her sense of sound and sight, the gentle lady said, "I'll just be so grateful that you come to visit." There was an uncommon freedom in that student's eyes as she told me of her friend. Somehow a great enemy had been disarmed in her life.

Gratitude not only empowers the receiver of the gift; it confirms the giver. "You really believe I love you," the giver says in the heart.

It is truly wondrous when others actually believe you love them. It is glorious when someone thanks you.

Might God be more interested in our gratitude than anything else? Was the primal sin ingratitude?

The healed leper, Naaman, proclaimed to Elisha, "Now I know there is no God in all the earth, except in Israel." How God must have delighted.

And Christ, having healed ten, saw something greater in the one Samaritan who made time to come back, fall at his feet, and praise God. He saw the splendor of a human heart that believes it is loved, that accepts the gift. Such faith not only brings salvation. It is the gift back to God, so enchanting that God would die for love of it.

TWENTY-NINTH SUNDAY IN ORDINARY TIME

51. Perseverance

Ex. 17:8–13; 2 Tim. 3:14–4:2; Lk. 18:1–8

"Remain faithful."

The image of Moses looking out over Joshua's battle with Amalek does not easily fade from the mind. There he leans, his back against a rock, outstretched arms propped up by two aides. Whenever Moses lowers his arms for rest, the enemy begins to prevail; so Aaron and Hur stay at his side until sunset and victory, living crutches for his aching shoulders.

Now that's persistence in prayer. Supposedly it is the kind of perseverance that Paul recommends for Timothy—and us all—in our living and giving of the faith. As long as we are laboring at faith, faith is winning. If we give up, faith loses. Therefore Paul advises Timothy to "preach the word, to stay with the task whether convenient or inconvenient, correcting, reproving, appealing, constantly teaching and never losing patience."

Ah, but those inconvenient times, those days when the battle seems to have no end. Who will prop up our arms when they are wearied with prayer? The distressing thought surfaces: Why even bother to keep the arms held high when it seems that our begging brings no relief?

Jesus told his disciples a parable on the necessity of praying always and not losing heart. A widow pleads before a corrupt judge for vindication against an opponent. Irritation rather than compassion finally moves the judge to help her. The only way to stop her complaining is to give in to her pleading.

And this is a corrupt judge. How different it is with a good and bountiful God, who has given us life. It is God's desire to help us when we call out by night and day; God is eager to answer our cries for help. Thus Jesus asks his hearers, "Will God delay long over them, do you suppose?"

But delay, by and large, is unfortunately what you experience. You wonder if you are even heard. Heaven seems at times to be wired like those labyrinthine voice-mail systems. You keep getting the runaround. You keep hitting the same buttons, hearing the same evasions.

I've spent over a year of days pleading for a miracle. I don't often do that, but the situation merits it. Show your power, O God, to the world. Manifest your love for one of your chosen, young and true, a woman good and generous, now wounded and needy of your assistance. If not now, when? If not here, where? As the days wear on, I fear not only that you delay, but that the plea might never be answered. I grow weary holding up her cause to you.

And this is the complaint of only one—one person in the sea of humanity—with one prayer seemingly unanswered. My little voice is lost in the roar of pleading that resounds through the ages. Families in desperate poverty and loss join the chorus. Chants rise from Dachau, requiems from Rwanda, dirges from the bloody wars, screams from the ghetto. Lost in the din of history is the weeping from battered children, abandoned souls, distraught minds. Who will prop up the outstretched arms of humanity, pained with almost endless ache?

Perhaps Jesus meant the story of the widow to represent the state of humanity itself, suffering in the wound of time. The very condition of our fallen creaturehood needs some final healing. All temporary cures, all wars won, all peace treaties are just signals. There is no earthly final therapy, no definitive victory over death, no endless peace.

The object of our belief is a God free of space's limit, of time's transience. It is the God who deemed us good and abides in that judgment beyond all the evidence we provide to the contrary. It is the God who made our outstretched arms his own in the crucified one, who even in crushing loss said, "Into your hands I commend my spirit."

What is required of us is to pray always. Our very being must be a prayer, a petition. What is asked of us is that we never lose heart; our very existence must become an act of trust.

There are, when it comes down to it, only two responses to our condition. We can give up hope in humanity and the God who fashioned us, or we can believe that the last word, beyond all our earthly disasters, is the word of love from the one who called us into existence.

Thus, for God incarnate a fundamental concern looms large. Christ asks but one thing of us: not that we comprise an invulnerable army, never wounded or pained, at the end of time, but that we form a vast cavalcade of men and women who, despite the sufferings of history, believe in his promise.

"When the Son of Man comes, will he find any faith on the earth?"

52. Self-Righteousness

Sir. 35:12–14, 16–18; 2 Tim. 4:6–8, 16–18; Lk. 18:9–14

"The prayer of the lowly pierces the clouds."

Ages ago, about this time of year, we used to go to church to pray for the poor souls in Purgatory. I can remember making multiple visits with my father. All Souls Day was a bargain day for indulgences, more opportune than a fire sale, where you could participate in the eternal liberation of some lost, perhaps totally forgotten spirit. We usually made three visits marked by five recitations of the Our Father, the Hail Mary and the Glory Be, each set interrupted by a smoke out on the steps of St. Magdalen's.

There may be loads of theological problems with this practice, but there was something wondrous about it. Behind the ritual was a great truth waiting to be felt. It had to do, first of all, with God. God actually wanted us to be saved, even if we got into terrible straits. The church provided this baroque system of rescue to remind us that God intended our escape from dire fate. Even the fact that we might mention the "soul who has no one to pray for her," or the "soul who has been in Purgatory for the longest time," was a way of entering some lavish scheme of forgiveness and care.

This practice is, for the most part, long gone. But the reality abides—as long as we have the holy book to remind us that our God hears the cry of the poor. "God is close to the broken-hearted; those crushed in spirit God saves." Thus does Psalm 34 echo the wisdom of Sirach: "Though not unduly partial to the weak, God hears the cry of the oppressed."

The holy souls, all those who know need, all those who know they are lost if they rely on their own powers, all those who know they cannot count on their own righteousness, are all we might aspire to be. Saints or sinners, no one of us is a self-made man or woman. To think so is a delusion. To want it is a false and dangerous dream.

Can you imagine telling a self-made woman that she is actually a sinner in need? Can you conceive of telling a self-made man that he is loved? They are unable to hear such things. They are preoccupied with their own achievements.

"I give you thanks, O God, that I am not like the rest of people—grasping, crooked, adulterous—or even like this tax collector. I fast twice a week, I pay tithes on all I possess." I made it. I have it made. I've earned it. The words may feel very good to say, but they slam tight the doors of reception and gift. The self-righteous do not need the righteousness of God. They do not need God's love. They need not ask for mercy. They want nothing from God. Perhaps they want nothing of God.

What is more, their lives are spent in comparison. Who is better, who is worse, who is first? And those who do not measure up to their canons of success are deemed unworthy. It was to such people, "who believed in their own self-righteousness, while holding everyone else in contempt," that Jesus spoke his parable.

Far behind the high and mighty man in front singing his own praises was a poor soul in the rear of the temple. He seemed to consider himself unworthy, keeping his distance. Was he a crook? An adulterer? Perhaps sad at his own failure, his eyes are lowered. The words are simple. "O God, be merciful to me, a sinner." He is heard and he can hear. There are no comparisons in his prayer, just the simple truth. It is he who goes home, not lost in his ego, but one with God.

The great and mighty Apostle Paul must have tasted this truth. What an achiever, what a worker he was. How great his triumphs. As we read in the Second Letter to Timothy, he "fought the good fight, finished the race and kept the faith." But the righteousness reserved for him was ultimately given by his rescuer, his savior. He did not achieve it himself.

The race run is also mentioned in the letter to the Philippians. Paul entered that race only after he realized that all his accomplishments were so much rubbish and that he could no longer aspire to perfection by his own effort. A faultless Pharisee, having given up the pretense of being a self-made man, Paul learned the freedom of the poor soul who one day, in the back of the temple, could only mutter, "Lord, have mercy."

And the Irish immigrant who brought his son on visits to the back of a church in St. Louis was living out a parable that Christ had spoken in earlier times. Enter the lives of the poor souls. You will find not only yourself there. You will also discover the mystery of God.

53. Zacchaeus

Wis. 11:22–12:1; 2 Thess. 1:11–2:2; Lk. 19:1–10

"I want to stay at your house."

Judging from the harsh things that Jesus said about wealth and privilege, we might reasonably think it well nigh impossible for a rich person not only to enter the gates of heaven, but also to come into the good graces of Jesus himself.

Zacchaeus was rich. A prominent tax collector, he even seemed to have suspicions about fraud in his own practices. He may have been small in stature, but he was definitely into big-time operations. It also happened that he wanted to see what Jesus was like. So, running ahead of a big crowd's rush, he climbed a sycamore to see what he could see.

It's an interesting scene—unlike my own imagined scenario. I would have the master, eyes aflame, look at the conniver and warn him of his impending doom. Jesus would then launch into a rousing condemnation of exploitation and injustice. Zacchaeus would serve as prime example. But the Christ of Luke's Gospel (a Gospel, mind you, that is one of the harshest in denouncing riches and the oppression of the poor) once again confounds expectations. "Zacchaeus, hurry down. I want to stay at your house."

Now I would have at least put some conditions on my visit. "Do you promise to turn away from your greedy behavior? Are you willing to abandon the errant ways of your business and lifestyle?" Why do these things not cross the mind of Jesus? He has preached about greed often enough. And here's a real live capitalist pig he could whale into; but instead, he asks to be invited home. Needless to say, Zacchaeus was thrilled. He welcomed Christ with delight.

I have to admit I would be among the murmurers. This tax-collecting creep has gone his merry way making his commission on the backs of the poor. Now, on a whim, he climbs up into a tree to see Jesus (whom all of us want to talk to and have been following for months), and he gets an interview. A money-grubber! The gang would support me in this. To think that Jesus is going to have dinner with the likes of Zacchaeus.

It is always fascinating to see how Jesus treats sinners, whether tax-collectors, liars, adulterers, or cowards. It's a wonder how he deals with them, how he deals with us all, how he deals with all things. Clearly, Jesus is interested in the energy and desire of the little man. He seems impressed by the fact that Zacchaeus would go to such lengths to see him and would eventually stand his ground before the daunting crowd. It is Zacchaeus's heart, his hope, that draws Jesus.

The fact that Christ liked him seemed to have an immediate effect on Zacchaeus. "I give half my belongings to the poor. . . . If I have defrauded anyone in the least I pay him back fourfold."

Even here, I think Christ was too soft. I would have said, "Only half? What about the other 50 percent? And what do you mean, 'If I have defrauded?' Be more specific." But no! Jesus announces salvation to the whole house of Zacchaeus and calls him, believe it or not, a "true son of Abraham." That's that. "The Son of Man has come to search out and save what was lost."

And so, once again, my paltry prudence, my so-called sense of justice, shrinks in the presence of wisdom, before whom the whole universe is as a grain of sand or a drop of morning dew on the earth. God, indeed, overlooks our sins so that we might repent and thereby change. Such is the manner of infinite mercy.

"For you love all things that are and loathe nothing that you have made; for what you hated, you would not have fashioned. How could a thing remain unless you willed it; or be preserved, had it not been called forth by you? You spare all things, because they are yours, O God and lover of souls." That goes for Zacchaeus. That goes for us too.

What the Book of Wisdom tells us is that we could not even exist if we were not loved by God. The very fact that we live without causing our own existence is proof that we are loved into being. We could not have been made, could not endure an instant, unless we were willed and wanted.

We brothers and sisters of Zacchaeus, more splendidly endowed than other creatures, have an extra gift. It is more desirable than the majesty of mountains, more thrilling than the speed of the finest gazelle. God, that lover of souls, wants, most of all, to spare that gift in us. It is the gift we share with Zacchaeus, no matter how rich or poor, how young or old, how virtuous or sinful we might be. We are gifted with a question at the ground of our being. And even in the worst of times, we climb trees to find out what the answer might be.

THIRTY-SECOND SUNDAY IN ORDINARY TIME

54. The Great Union

2 Macc. 7:1–2, 9–14; 2 Thess. 2:16–3:5; Lk. 20:27–38

"All are alive for God."

C. S. Lewis wrote *The Great Divorce* as a rebuttal to those who think that heaven and hell are not radically incompatible. Blake's "Marriage of Heaven and Hell" suggests to us, Lewis claimed, that good and evil are somehow blurred. At least they're not contradictory. But for Lewis this was not the case. Evil can be repented, but it can never evolve into good. Our fate is a matter of either/or, a question of where our hearts find their final treasure. More precisely, heaven or hell is the result of how we define ourselves while on earth. There may be a great divorce between heaven and hell, but there is a great union between our life on earth and our eternal destiny.

The story of the seven Maccabees and their mother says as much. These brothers were arrested and tortured to death. One of the sons, who was skinned alive, said to his tormentors, "You are depriving us of this present life, but the King of the world will raise us up to live again forever." A second brother, before his tongue was cut out and he was dismembered, proclaimed that he died with the confidence of being "whole again." Yet another found courage in divine providence, the "God-given hope of being restored."

The Maccabees became at their death, for all eternity, what they loved most. As they died, so they eternally would live, in love and fidelity. This is why their mother could encourage them: "I do not know how you appeared in my womb; it was not I who endowed you with life and breath; I had not the shaping of your every part. It is the creator of the world, ordaining the process of birth and presiding over the origin of all things, who in his mercy will most surely give you back breath and life."

Life after death also preoccupied the Sadducees, who apparently did not believe in the resurrection of the dead, when they put their questions to Jesus. A man dies, leaving a widow. His brother marries her. This little scenario is repeated until seven brothers have married the woman. The Sadducees want to know who will be her husband in heaven. "Remember, seven married her."

Christ's response is that in the life to come there will be no marriage. "They become like angels and are no longer liable to death. God is not the God of the dead but of the living. All are alive for God."

But a question remains unanswered. What is the nature of the relationship between the resurrected life and this present one? What is the connection?

Some people (we may call them "supernatural dualists") seem to think there is a profound discontinuity between this life and the afterlife. We must choose between being happy in this world or in the next. It is hell, one might ironically think, all the way to heaven: misery, unhappiness, and unfulfillment now, but big rewards later. This life is the pilgrimage, the vale of tears, the test. The next life brings the reversal of roles.

Others (we might call natural humanists) seem to agree that there is a radical difference between earth and heaven. But they say we should choose the earth. As the "Humanist Manifesto" proposed, we ought to live this life without heavenly crutches or the promise of reward. In its stronger formulations, the naturalist approach looks upon heaven as "pie in the sky," or, as one well-known troublemaker put it, "the opiate of the people."

There is, however, a third option. What if there is no discontinuity between this life and the afterlife? What if there is just life, some of it eternal, some of it temporal? If that is the case, then the way we live now is the way we will always live. How we live is the promise of our destiny.

In this option, God does not threaten us with hell. We fashion it for ourselves by the choices we make: enclosed, egocentric, untrue, uncaring, unloving. That's a hellishly mean existence, whether in this life or the next.

Thus, as we live and die, so we become eternally, outside the limits of space and time. There may not be marriage in the afterlife, but there is the fulfillment of what we have been becoming. All of us, from the moment we begin, are endowed with an openness to God. But those of us who live long enough to exercise our freedom actually take part in determining our fate.

Like the Maccabees, we become what we have most loved, most believed, most hoped.

Thus, Lewis's fascinating parable of *The Great Divorce* is a story of people confronted with the deepest choices they make. Those who cling to their fears, who hug for dear life their resentments, who refuse to let go of their prisons, can only be given what they endlessly demand. Those, however, who give their lives in hope and trust, who cast themselves into the arms of the living God, no matter what their shame or sorrow, find what their hearts desired.

They encounter not only the graces of the earth and the faces of the beloved, but also the one in whom they lived, moved, and had their very being.

55. The End of the Ages

Mal. 3:19–20; 2 Thess. 3:7–12; Lk. 21:5–19

"The day will come."

Devastation. Ruin. Emptiness. Is this the fate of the earth? Was Bertrand Russell right when he prophesied that our origin, growth, and maturation would come to nothing? An honest philosophy, he claimed, could not reasonably deny that "no fire, no heroism, no intensity of thought and feeling can preserve an individual life beyond the grave. All the labours of the ages, all the devotion, all the inspiration, all the noonday brightness of human genius are destined to extinction in the vast death of the solar system." The great temple of human achievement would inevitably be reduced to debris in universal ruin.

Russell was a prophet without a savior, an apocalyptic mind that could not imagine a second coming. The prophet Malachi, centuries earlier, foresaw the same doom, the global blast-furnace where all pride and evil are reduced to rubble, where cancerous growth is uprooted and burned away. But Malachi saw hope; he believed the God who promised a new sun of justice with its healing rays.

As we lurch toward the year 2000, an opera of prophets will take the big stage. Apocalyptic literature will boom, even if the earth doesn't. Movies, self-help books, bogus practitioners of religio-craft, best sellers, and talk shows will buzz with anticipation. But it won't be anything new.

Jesus himself, in Luke's Gospel, saw terrible times ahead, a day coming when not one stone of our human temple will rest on another. He warned of the signs. There will be wars and insurrections. Nations will fight to the death against nations. Tribes, peoples, and clans will clash. The earth will protest with mighty quakes, the biosystem will spawn plague and famine. The sky will blossom with omens. Finally, there will be rejection and even persecution for those who believe in Christ.

I, however, have a question for the Lord. Has there ever been an age without such trial and turmoil? What century has not seen wars? What nation has not tried to bulldoze its way ahead of others—if not for victory in military struggle, at least for more respectable signs of gain? When have we not been plagued by cancerous life or tossed by mighty movements of earth and sea? And has there ever been a time when a true Christian has not been ridiculed and rejected, whether by friends, family, or state?

Just wondering.

Yet Christ, seeming to anticipate our wonder, offered this advice: "Do not be perturbed. . . . These things are bound to happen." Bound to happen. Life is bound to be this way. He is not speaking about the end of all times, but the condition of every time.

I believe there is at least one interpretation of apocalyptic literature (one far more solid than the endless announcements of the end of the world, based on occult reading of scripture) that takes such passages as revelations not so much of what is to come, but of what is now the case.

Each day is the last. Each time is the end time. Each human being faces the end of the world in the span of a life, whether it reach eight minutes or eighty years. The world, its opportunities and losses, passes away for us each night. Every sunset announces a closing of a day that will never come again. Each human death, as Russell pondered, is the curtain on an unrepeatable drama, which, without God, amounts to a tragedy. Every generation, in some way, is the last, the termination.

And each generation, like each death and every day, witnesses the signs of the end times.

Everything that Christ predicted has taken place and is taking place and will continue to take place. We need not wait until the millennium or turn to Nostradamus to unlock the mystery. Life itself is the mystery, this great groaning of creation that finds its meaning in hope alone.

Russell knew this. And since he had no hope, he saw all of human history, when all is said and done, as a cruel joke.

For those who hope, it is otherwise. As Paul writes in his Letter to the Romans, that groaning of all creation is an act of giving birth. "We, too, groan inwardly as we wait for our bodies to be set free. For we must be content to hope that we shall be saved."

And so Christ counsels us not to be alarmed at our condition. Do not follow the false messiahs and easy predictors. Words and wisdom will be given. Through all the turmoil of our days, our generation, our species, it is not death, but a new saving birth which is assured. In some final sense, "not a hair of your head will be harmed." In patient endurance, life will be saved. We await, then the arrival. "O Come, O Come," will be our prayer.

56. The Counter-Cultural Sovereign

2 Sam. 5:1–3; Col. 1:12–20; Lk. 23:35–43

"We are only paying the price for what we've done, but this man has done nothing wrong."

The Feast of Christ the King stands in stark opposition to two contemporary trends in some Christian circles. The first trend is the rejection of honorific titles like "king" or "lord." The

second is the proposal that Christ is not pre-eminent as a revelation of God, but merely one among many equal sources of
truth and salvation.

The distaste that some Christians have for the notion of
kingship mistakes the very nature of Christ's dominion. His is
a total reversal of the roles usually assigned to royalty and
servitude. He refuses to be the master of the world, the mighty
monarch, the spiller of blood. His reign subverts our notion of
kingship.

He is the king who serves the other. He is the king who dies
for the other. He is the king who is ridiculed, scorned, and
mocked. Most insufferable, most repugnant of all, is the fact
that he is a powerless sovereign. Dying on his cross-throne,
Jesus is thrice taunted for the fact that he does not save himself.
"You a savior?" they jeer. "Then save yourself." Soldiers with
their sour wine chide, "Aren't you a real king? Save yourself."
Even a criminal scolds: "I thought you were supposed to be a
Messiah. Prove it."

As opposed to every other king, Christ is unguarded. He
disavows the protection of armies. He rejects self-defense. He
abjures force. This is a king? No, this is a scandal. This is a
stumbling block. Thus, to repress Christ's title of king is to
repress the earth-shaking revolution of his realm. The crucified
king is also the secret key to Christ's uniqueness. There is none
other like him in the fables of human consciousness. No cult
or culture could dream it.

The mystery of the Cross is so difficult for humans to com-
prehend that even Christians have devoted their lives and
scholarship to ignoring the awful truth of Christ's sovereignty.
Christ's kingship is an abomination for any earthly royal aspi-
ration. It is an assault upon the desires of every tribe or nation
that ever craved ascendancy. More baffling yet, Christ the
king, utterly innocent, completely accepts the appearances of
utter guilt. One of the criminals crucified with him saw and
embraced this startling truth—and he was saved. "We deserve
it after all. We are only paying the price for what we've done,
but this man has done nothing wrong."

In celebrating Christ the King at the end of the church year, we force ourselves to remember the appalling fact of our salvation. God has spoken, become enfleshed Word, in a way that defies human cleverness. Our hunger for pre-eminence, our desire for dominance, which may well motivate our every choice and predilection, is spurned by this king.

René Girard, professor of language and culture at Stanford University, is a rare contemporary thinker who confronts the implications of Christian faith. In his book *Things Hidden Since the Foundation of the World*, Girard shows how Christ dismantles the triangle of desire, violence, and retribution. In Christ there is no envy, greed, or lust for power. He, the innocent king who executes none, is executed. He seeks no vengeance. Christ the king is the only sovereign to embody such principles.

Girard comments:

> It can be shown, I believe, that there is not a single action or word attributed to Jesus—including those that seem harshest at first sight—that is not consistent with the rule of the Kingdom. It is absolute fidelity to the principle defined in his own preaching that condemns Jesus. There is no other cause for his death than the love of one's neighbor lived to the very end.

He goes on to say that when we acknowledge Christ as God and king we accept his reversal of the violence that dominates humanity. "A non-violent deity can only signal his existence to mankind by having himself driven out by violence in the Kingdom of Violence."

Jesus is the sole king who saves fallen humanity from its twisted wish. In this respect he is truly original, truly exceptional, the divine challenge to a world which imagines kingship to be enslavement of the other. How appropriate it is, then, that St. Paul's letter to the Colossians professes Christ's cosmic centrality paradoxically revealed in the triumph of a cross. "He is the image of the invisible God, the first-born of all creatures. In him everything in heaven and on earth was created, things visible and invisible. . . . In him everything continues in being. . . . He is the beginning, the first-born of the dead, so that primacy may be his in everything. It pleased God to make absolute fullness reside in him and, by means of him, to reconcile everything in his person, everything, I say, both on earth and in the heavens, making peace through the blood of his cross."